CLASSROOMS THAT WORK

CLASSROOM

PRESCRIPTION

A Sunrise Book

THAT WORK

OR CHANGE

*Paul Graubard and
Harry Rosenberg*

E. P. DUTTON & CO., INC. · NEW YORK · 1974

Library of Congress Cataloging in Publication Data

Graubard, Paul S.
  Classrooms that work.

  "A Sunrise book."
  1. Exceptional children—Education.   I. Rosenberg,
  Harry Ewing, 1932–   joint author.   II. Title.
  LC3965.G75   371.9   74-4157

Dutton-Sunrise, Inc., a subsidiary of E. P. Dutton & Co., Inc.

First Edition

10 9 8 7 6 5 4 3 2 1

Published simultaneously in Canada by Clarke, Irwin & Company Limited,
Toronto and Vancouver
ISBN: 0-87690-131-3
Designed by The Etheredges

This book is dedicated to our wives,
Joy and Pat,
and to our children:
Risa, Aimee, Michael, David; and
Larry, Ann, Mary, Robert.
We hope that our children, and all children,
will be able to attend schools
that they respect and work
with teachers who respect them.

P.S.G. *and* H.E.R.

Contents

Acknowledgments

A special thanks goes to Larry Smith and Jerry Hausman for their editorial assistance. Dr. Martin Miller of Yeshiva University contributed to the ideation of this book and has been a rigorous critic of our work. Dr. Don Bushell, Jr., of the University of Kansas provided us with models of how schools can work and gave thorough criticism to a draft of the manuscript, as did Dr. Daniel O'Leary of the State University of New York at Stony Brook. John Tugman also gave us criticism and support and we are grateful to him. Charlotte Cook, Bobby and Carolyn Boss and Naomi Barber were also very helpful in criticizing the manuscript, as was Mr. Bernard Gerr, principal of C.S. 6 in the Bronx, New York. We are grateful to Dr. Bill Rhodes of the University of Michigan for his contribution to our thinking about deviant children.

Special thanks also go to Dr. Bluma Weiner, chairwoman of the Department of Special Education at Yeshiva University and to Dr. Katie LeLaurin and Mrs. Aileen Stan of the department. Arlene Rabinowitz, Jo Anne Vale, Carolyn Smith, Joseph Kovaly, Linda Forman, and Arlene Markow, graduate students at Yeshiva University, also criticized various portions of the manuscript.

We are also grateful to Doug Lovik, Newell Herum, and Bob Morgan from the Visalia Unified School District (California) for their support and assistance. Tom Clifford, Dick Ehrgott, and Guy Chapman were also most helpful. Jim Moore, Cliff Denham, Chuck Richmond, and Richard Rasner did a good deal of the work with children and they did an outstanding job. Heidi Leibowitz edited the chapter notes and references.

Marye Meyers did the final typing of the manuscript.

Marian Skedgell of E. P. Dutton & Company first suggested the book, and she has proved to be an ideal editor. We are very grateful to her.

Thanks also go to Risa and Aimee Graubard for their reading of the manuscript. Many of the incidents described in this book are a reflection of their school experiences. Finally, there is especially an appreciation for the help of Joy Graubard. She not only helped with the manuscript and held family and home together, but also provided a special kind of support and love. The book never would have been written without her.

P.S.G. *and* H.E.R.

1

Children Who Need Help

An ideal educational system should be able to help *every* child. Conversely, educational systems should not have to reject *any* child. An important goal for schools to strive toward is one in which no child is given a second-class education and every child achieves minimum competencies and positive feelings of self-worth.

Almost every class has one child who needs special help, and most classes have even more. In some sections of the country whole classes have achievement levels and behavior patterns that are more akin to those of special classes than to those of regular classes. Special-education children and their teachers also need help. Principals and guidance counselors know these special children and special classes well. Teachers and administrators spend an inordinate amount of time with them, searching desperately for programs and methods to help these children and at the same time make their own lives more bearable.

The problems of the child with learning and behavior difficulties are so great in terms of his and his parents' suffering, not to mention that of the teacher, and the burden is so great on the taxpayer, that an important criterion in judging the effectiveness of schools is how well they succeed in reducing this deviant or exceptional behavior.

Some educators might complain that the reduction of deviancy is not a fair criterion by which to judge schools, arguing that deviant behavior is caused by genetic and environmental conditions over which the schools have no control. True, much deviant behavior is caused by genetic and home conditions, but the school *can* control what happens within its own boundaries.

With the tools of behavior modification, it is now possible to help children far more effectively than has been possible in the past. Teachers can increase the academic skills of special children and teach them social behaviors that will decrease the likelihood of their getting into trouble. This can be done for less money and with greater efficiency than in traditional approaches. We cannot continue business-as-usual with these children, because our current methods have not worked in the past and will not work in the future.

Let us consider how behavior-modification methods helped one child, Tommy, a fourth-grader in an urban school system. Tommy's mother died when he was six. He had never really known his father. Tommy's aunt and uncle, a couple well into their sixties, took him in after his mother's death, but they were unable to control his behavior.

In school, Tommy was almost a nonreader and he exploded in frustration during his reading periods. He was constantly in fights and had once been suspended for throwing a chair at a teacher. Tommy had received play therapy since first grade, but his behavior had not improved. The school administrators had tried to put Tommy into a special class, but there was no room for him there. After his fourth-grade teacher refused to work with Tommy he was put on half-day sessions and transferred to another class.

His new teacher had a great deal of difficulty working with him. Tommy would enter the class on his hands and knees and crawl around the room during academic periods. He would groan and shout for no apparent reason and often bullied smaller children. He did quite well in arithmetic but refused even to attend his reading sessions. His new teacher went home in tears several times during his first weeks in her class and considered resigning rather than trying to work with Tommy.

She went to the social worker and learned all about Tommy's home life and about the dynamics that the social worker considered important. The teacher did not learn what to do with him specifically, however, and in desperation she asked a behavioral psychologist for help in working with Tommy.

The behavioral psychologist helped the teacher to set up concrete goals or minimal expectancies for Tommy, goals that were realistic for him, given his present level of functioning. The goals had to be overt and capable of being measured. "Changing his attitude toward school" was rejected as being too ambiguous. "Walking upright" and "sitting in his seat during reading lessons" were accepted. Both the quantity and quality that would be considered acceptable in his work were made explicit, and specific rewards were attached to his achieving the goals that were worked out with him.

At the beginning of Tommy's new program, the

teacher kept a frequency count of Tommy's unacceptable behaviors. These records were shared with him and additional rewards were tied to a reduction of these behaviors. The rewards ranged from going out for coffee for the teacher during the lunch break and thereby earning a ten-cent tip, to going to the zoo on a Saturday afternoon. (The latter reward nearly got the teacher into trouble with the visiting psychiatrist and social worker, who felt that the teacher was "overidentifying" with Tommy, and it was only on the aunt's insistence that Tommy was allowed to earn this reward.) The class was given the opportunity to share some of these rewards. The teacher instructed the class to ignore Tommy's inappropriate behavior and to help him learn academic skills. When Tommy reduced his inappropriate behavior to an explicit degree, both the class and Tommy received an extra gym period.

The teacher also revised Tommy's reading curriculum. Instead of working in a textbook, they played Grab (a form of Go Fish with sight vocabulary words), and a reward was placed on Tommy's learning each new word. They played this game so that Tommy could get used to working with the teacher in academic situations and so that the teacher would have a better understanding of Tommy's strengths and weaknesses in reading. The teacher later used a set of remedial reading drills that were not in text form. The format of the material lent itself to short work sessions and the time of the lessons was increased quite gradually. The lessons were sequential and were set up in such a way that Tommy could see his progress. For every page completed with more than 80 percent accuracy Tommy earned a point, and these points were later cashed in for his trip to the zoo or other rewards.

The teacher worked with Tommy's strengths instead

of concentrating on his weaknesses. Even though Tommy's obstreperous behavior created such emotional turmoil that it was difficult to accept his positive behaviors, the teacher gave him positive reinforcement during those times of the day when he was quiet and cooperative. She also accepted him as a person and let him know that she liked many of his behaviors. These included his sense of humor, his athletic skills and ability to organize games, and the responsibility and competence he showed when he took care of the plants in the classroom.

The behavior-modification system proved to be successful in that Tommy did learn reading skills, and he began to behave more appropriately in school. These changes did not occur overnight; they were the result of weeks and even months of patient work on the part of the teacher. During that period Tommy had many setbacks and the teacher experienced a great deal of frustration. Nevertheless, the trend was clear.

Tommy stopped going to the social worker because he found the sessions "boring" and he preferred reading. He also behaved well enough in school so that when an opening occurred in the special class the school administration and the teacher no longer felt it was necessary to place him there. He resumed going to school a full day and continued to make progress. Tommy was also promoted to the fifth grade at the end of the year.

Behavior modification has been used to treat deviant behavior, but unlike the psychotherapeutic approach to deviancy, behavior modification deals with manifest behavior, believing that if the "symptom" is cured the disease itself is cured. The behavior-modification approach does not examine the past for causative explanations of a child's behavior. A basic premise of behavior modification is that while behavior is determined by experiences in the past, human behavior is so complex and our history of any individual is so incomplete that the "whys" of any human behavior can never be fully comprehended.

Those who practice behavior modification first ask themselves, "What specific behaviors do I want to accelerate or decelerate?" and then they seek in the environment those stimuli which will maintain, strengthen, or weaken behaviors, and for consequences in the environment that will serve to suppress, extinguish, or develop specific behaviors. In the school environment, if a child is not capable of the terminal behavior that is desired, behavior modification practitioners will then reinforce successive approximations to the desired behavior. For example, if a child cannot read, he will be taught to match letters to sounds and sound out words, and so forth, until the terminal behavior (reading) has been learned.

A key to the behavior-modification approach to teaching can be found in the word *contingency*. Reinforcers or consequences are delivered to the pupil *contingent* upon a particular behavior. Then a careful analysis is made of the behavior and the effects, if any, that the contingency has had on that behavior. When objective data show a functional relationship between a particular contingency and a particular behavior, the contingency is manipulated to accelerate or decelerate the behavior.

Token economies, a system based on these behavior modification and reinforcement principles, have been widely used with deviant children and with "normal" children as well, with such remarkable success that two research psychologists who reviewed the literature in the field were unable to find one case of a token-economy system that had not succeeded in changing children's behavior. While generally only successful cases are reported in the literature, these procedures have been replicated so many times that any failure to do so would most probably have been noted.

In a token system a unit of exchange such as a poker chip, gold star, or other retainable symbol is awarded to a child by the behavior modifier, contingent upon a specific response. Such tokens then take on the properties of conditioned reinforcers when they are exchanged for a backup reinforcer that can be selected by the child from among several items. To predict just what items will work as reinforcers for any particular child is difficult, and the problem of children shifting desires or wants is avoided in a token economy, since the tokens can purchase numerous items. Token economies are usually initiated when more natural kinds of reinforcers such as praise or grades do not shape or maintain a behavior. Thus a token economy serves to bridge the gap between the building of the behavior and its maintenance by "natural" consequences.

The token-economy procedures, and other behavior-modification techniques, can be objectively evaluated and replicated. They do not depend on the charismatic qualities of the teacher.

Behavior modification has been developed into a powerful and explicit technology. The basic research methodology of behavior modification de-emphasizes studies that base their conclusions on correlations, or the finding that a relationship appears to exist between a given method and a change in behavior. Behaviorists argue that such a relationship might well be fortuitous. Instead, they rely on data that show that the procedures can *produce* changes in behavior, much akin to the rules of the physical sciences. To judge whether a particular behavior-modification study adds to the technology of teaching, the criterion used is that a typically well-trained reader should be able to replicate the procedure and produce the same results merely from having read the procedure.

Besides the use of contingencies, an equally important aspect of the behavior-modification approach can be found in the word *measurement*. The behavior modifier must precisely define what behavior is to be changed. This behavior must be observable, unambiguous, and capable of being counted. The practitioner then counts the number of occurrences of this behavior in a given time span. This is done before any intervention procedure is used, and it is called the baseline. The baseline can be self-recorded or recorded by others. The counts can be as simple as putting slash marks on a sheet of paper whenever the given behavior occurs. To ensure objectivity, behaviorists prefer that an independent rater corroborate the occurrence of the behavior.

The next step is for the contingencies or the intervention to be applied. Counts are then taken on the same behavior, and any change is noted. The procedures that were in effect during the initial counting (or baseline period) are then reinstituted and counts are again taken and compared so that changes can be attributed to the procedures and not to chance. In other words, behavior modification researchers want to find out if the procedure used can actually change the behavior in question. If the procedure can produce behavioral changes it can probably be used by other teachers in different settings and get the same results.

The law of gravity is in effect whether we are aware of it or not. Similarly, according to behaviorists, human behavior is affected, either being strengthened or weakened, by the responses that follow the behavior in question. Behavior that an individual finds rewarding is likely to be repeated, and behavior that is ignored will decrease or become extinct. Measurement can make clear what effect particular responses have upon behavior, and what kinds of interventions are effective.

Dr. Don Bushell, a leading behavioral sociologist, once stated that great breakthroughs in science have been preceded by advances in measurement. Our ability to control disease was limited for hundreds of thousands of years. Once Leeuwenhoek developed the microscope, medical scientists made rapid and effective advances against the organisms producing disease. Probably more knowledge has been accumulated to fight disease in the three hundred years since the utilization of the microscope than in the thousands of years preceding this important invention.

It has only been within the last few decades that we have been able to measure behavior directly, without reference to norms or other indirect criteria. Because we can now directly measure an individual's behavior, we can understand what controls that behavior and how to manipulate those controls to change the behavior. Behaviorists use the word *control* of behavior to signify an *understanding* of the functional relationship between a behavior and the environmental events which surround that behavior. They do not mean control in the sense of repression. As a result of this control, many autistic children who would have lived their lives in isolation from the world have been taught to communicate. Many children who would formerly have had speech defects have been taught to speak clearly. The quality of life has been improved for many children because of these scientific advances.

Science does not tell us what *should be;* it tells us what *is.* We have to decide for ourselves what should be and then use the tools of science and technology to reach our goals. In education, we must be more explicit about what behaviors we want to strengthen and what behaviors we want to decrease, so that educators and technologists can help us get there.

Our society cannot afford to reject talents and skills. We have found that racial segregation and the denial of equal educational opportunity cost us too much in wasted lives and broken dreams. The cost to our society in failing to solve the problems of the child with learning and behavior difficulties is equally high. In like measure we cannot continue to deny teachers the help they need to work more effectively with such children.

CHILDREN AS DEVIANTS

Who defines what behaviors are deviant is as crucial a question in reducing deviancy as is the question of which behaviors are to be accelerated or decelerated. These questions are best answered *directly*, for if they are not, it is too easy to get sidetracked. Some of the assumptions that lie behind our perceptions of deviancy and some of the current practices based on these assumptions hinder the development of effective programs.

A child is usually considered deviant or exceptional when he or she does not live up to the expectations of those who have power. For children to be considered deviant, they must display behavior that the perceiver considers inappropriate—that is, behavior that the perceiver wishes stopped. When a child violates the perceiver's situational definition of appropriate behavior, he is not acting the role that the perceiver expects.

Many behaviors that children engage in, such as daydreaming or playing, are often deemed appropriate in a home environment, while in the school environment they are inappropriate, punishable, or at the very least ignorable. Behaviors in and of themselves are neither good nor bad, neither healthy nor pathological. From the relativist point of view, terms such as "pathological," "non-normative," and "social deviant" are equivalent, and the behavior in question can best be examined in terms of (1) the specific behavior, (2) the effect of the behavior upon the perceiver, and (3) the perception of the behavior by the behaver. Examining the interaction between behavers in a given environment instead of examining the individual's behaviors independently of their context can be called the ecological approach.

RELATIVITY AND SOCIAL DEVIANCY

The ecological model of social deviancy derives from studies such as those of anthropologist Ruth Benedict, who as long ago as 1934 noted the ease with which people who in the United States might be considered abnormal or even dangerous were entirely functional in their own cultures. In certain Melanesian tribes, for example, normative behavior was found to include the expectation that anyone might try to kill another; therefore, to accept food prepared by anyone but a close member of one's family would be unthinkable. In such a culture anyone observed as open and trusting would also be considered deviant. No matter what kinds of "abnormality" Benedict observed, ranging from extreme instability to behaviors more in the form of character traits, such as acquisitiveness, sadism, or susceptibility to addiction, there were always well-established cultures in which people so afflicted by American standards could function with ease.

In the social deviancy model, selected behaviors, which can be almost any behaviors, are defined as deviant by a group wielding power within a society; the manifest behavior is less important to the definition than is the fact that certain taboos have been broken or that there has been a violation of the culture's expectations, creating an agitated exchange between the culture violator and the culture upholder. The notion of aberrant or maladaptive behavior (often called, in our society, emotional disturbance) can be reasonably interpreted in different ways: in the language of psychopathology that is popular now or in the language of learning theory, which states that so-called normal as well as so-called abnormal behaviors have been learned.

Many of the situations surrounding emotional disturbance—one form of social deviancy—can be compared to board games such as Monopoly. Much of the process and most of the outcome depend on which square one lands on, how much money one has in the "bank," and how good one is at bargaining and making the best deal. However, a big difference between being designated "emotionally disturbed" and Monopoly is that, in the former case, not all players begin with an equal number of opportunities. In the emotional-disturbance game, certain players, depending on social class, IQ, verbal skill, or other factors, are more likely to "Go to jail" or draw cards that create problems, such as "Pay a tax" or "Go back three squares," while others are inheriting money or landing on squares that allow them to build houses on Park Place.

To make clear not only this analogy but also the ecological approach to emotional disturbance, imagine that a child has absented himself from school for fifty days of an eighty-day school term. If located by school authorities, such a child usually enters the system through a door that says "clinical," and a guidance counselor or clinical psychologist will most likely apply a medical label to him. He will be viewed and then designated as "sick" or "emotionally disturbed" and will be considered in need of psychological treatment. The same child might also be viewed as a "juvenile delinquent" or "person in need of supervision" and his school will send him to the dean of discipline or probation officer. To the members of a counterculture, however, his act of skipping school could be considered laudable, or perhaps only normal. The same action, viewed by a sociologist, could be thought of as "learned behavior of a subculture that is at variance with the larger or dominant culture's mores." How the behavior is labeled and society's reaction to the child and that label are very much a matter of chance.

Labels denote sets of expectations that the society in general, and guilds in particular (psychiatry, social work, special education, correctional officialdom, etc.), maintain for those who are labeled.

THE EFFECTIVENESS OF LABELS

The phenomenon of the self-fulfilling prophecy has great relevance for the treatment of deviance. The self-fulfilling prophecy is in the beginning a false definition of a situation, leading to behaviors that make the original false conception come true. If a child is labeled a thief and everyone in his environment treats him like one, he will probably begin to steal. His reasoning might be that since everyone is going to blame him for thievery, what difference would it make if he actually steals something? Children who are called schizophrenic are treated differently from children who are not given that label. While a specific behavior might lead to a child's being labeled, in practice the whole child is categorized and dealt with according to the label imposed by the mental health practitioners.

The effect of labels has been demonstrated in a number of studies, ranging from the perception of rats' behaviors running mazes to academic achievement in ethnic minorities. While some of these studies have been criticized on methodological grounds and it is necessary to extrapolate beyond the data provided, there does appear to be a Pygmalion effect working, which can either benefit or harm those who are labeled. Labels can also do terrible damage to feelings of self-worth. It has clearly been documented that an essential part of the lives of those who have been labeled "retarded" is spent in trying to avoid that stigma and in denying to themselves and to others that it had once been their label.

Dr. Jane Mercer, a sociologist from the University of California, quotes one mother as saying, "There is nothing wrong with Benny . . . he just can't read or write." Since the mother spoke only broken English, had no formal education, and could not read or write, Benny did not appear deviant to her. Nor did he appear deviant to many of his friends and relatives. In fact, a substantial body of research shows that, after leaving school, most children who are labeled as retarded meld into the general community and are not behaviorally very different from their peers in the same social class.

The medical model of deviancy, which is generally used as a tool in our educational system, views mental retardation and/or emotional disturbance as primarily a physical condition. Mercer describes the results of this approach succinctly: "We say that a person *is* mentally retarded with the clear implication that mental retardation is a condition that exists *in* that person. Implicit in this viewpoint is the assumption that mental retardation can be present in a person although undetected. That it is a condition which can exist independent of its being identified and labeled, just as a case of rheumatic fever can exist undiagnosed."

However, a considerable amount of research tells us that "mental retardation" and "emotional disturbance" do not exist independently of the perceiver (or labeler), since both these phenomena are only discovered or acted upon in accordance with cultural norms. That is to say, such phenomena can be understood only in a context of social behavior within a social system, where there are shared expectations of how people should play their roles. A child given the status "student" is expected to play the role of learning and satisfying a teacher. By playing the role properly, the child allows the teacher to do the same.

In a California school district, Mercer has traced the steps necessary to "become" mentally retarded. The first step is to be conscripted into the public school system. The second step is to be perceived as deviant within that system. Once perceived as deviant, the child can then, at the option of the teacher, *earn* such classifications as "unearned social promotion" or "academic problem," either of which might cause the child to be referred to mental health professionals. A child can gain access to special education facilities by being labeled a "reading problem" or "underachiever" or "speech problem" without losing the status of regular student, but any of these labels initiated by teachers may expose the student to evaluation by the mental health team, who will use clinical judgments based on psychometric instruments to decide if the child is "disturbed," "retarded," or testing low enough to be placed in a "special class." Mercer found that while many children might have been labeled "retarded," few were.

We can find in Mercer's California study an indication that the medical perspective toward mental retardation pervades community programs and institutions. In the context of schools, the basic definitions of the medical perspective state that any child not conforming to the rules or mastering the curriculum is deviant. The curriculum is not put into question, nor are the rules. The onus is put on the child—not on the teacher, not on the school, not on the system.

THE MEDICAL MODEL

A negative effect of labeling and the medical model as used in schools is that the child can be reinforced for behavior that one wants to extinguish. A basic tenet of behavioral psychology is that behavior which is reinforced tends to recur and, in fact, to be strengthened by such reinforcement. Since the medical model concerns itself with pathology, it is often the "pathological" behavior itself that is reinforced in the course of treatment.

An example of this is reported by Dr. Edgar Auerswald. Auerswald writes about Maria, a twelve-year-old Puerto Rican girl in New York City, who was hospitalized as a schizophrenic. Her public school described Maria as a slow, steady learner who was detached from other children in the school. She was also described as likable, and able to get along well with other children in an afterschool group where she gave a very positive impression. Maria was undergoing treatment by a local child-guidance center because of a history of cutting classes and running away from home, and one time when Maria ran away the guidance center reported her absence to the police.

Found late at night on the streets by police, the girl was committed to an adolescent psychiatric ward of a large New York City hospital. Her behavior on the ward alternated between childish manipulation and a seductive behavior appearing bizarre in a twelve-year-old. In the light of her repeated runaways from home, her therapists felt that the girl should be kept in a situation where the running away would be alleviated and her therapy continued. In other words, since the girl was "sick," they felt that only a hospital could treat her.

The medically oriented therapists removed Maria from the only system that could engender growth and socialization—the family, the school, and the community—which would provide the experience she needed to participate in her society. They also succeeded in stamping a label on her history—that of childhood schizophrenic—a label that is extremely ambiguous to scientists and diagnosticians, but which to the lay public simply means "crazy."

On the other hand, an ecologically oriented therapist, who had become aware of the case during the police search for Maria, chose to examine the context of the girl's life. This therapist found that Maria's sister admitted, with some noticeable relish, to knowing where Maria had gone during her runaway periods; she had been mascot for a group of older boys with whom she often traveled for several days at a time. While the sister did not profess to know exactly what happened during the escapades, she suspected that sex was involved. Neither Maria's sister nor her mother really seemed to know much about Maria's personal life; they suggested that her grandfather might know more about her.

The grandfather obviously cared a great deal for Maria and he bemoaned the lack of understanding that existed in her home.

Within five hours, using an ecological approach, therapists constructed a picture of a child who had grown up in relative isolation, in a fatherless home. Communication between Maria and her mother had dwindled over the years, probably due to her older sister's attempts to maintain her own favored position in the home. Maria had then turned to her grandfather, who was himself isolated in his marriage, and in equal need of warmth and compassion.

Maria's history showed that she responded readily in small groups where she could identify with someone who liked her, such as the group worker at her school. Still, it was apparent that her methods of gaining a response from others were limited to infantile techniques of manipulation, or to using sex. The ecologically oriented therapist recommended a treatment plan alternative to the psychotherapeutic one that had been unsuccessfully tried. The recommendation called for changing the systems within which Maria's patterns of behavior appeared sick or crazy and changing the patterns of reinforcement that she received. The girl could then learn new coping patterns, since she would be operating within *systems* that had undergone change. An effort to reestablish communication between the mother and Maria would be attempted. In addition, the group worker's investment in the girl could be used to good effect. In other words, rather than the original therapists' concern with pathology, concentration could be placed on helping the family to work with the girl. Unfortunately, the medical therapist who was in charge of the case could not accept this system of thinking. He decided that Maria should remain in the hospital. There, all the attention she received depended upon her cutting school and staying away from home.

Another instance of the medical model's ignoring the surrounding system is found in the case of Jimmy, a boy who was labeled schizophrenic and expelled from school on the grounds that he was insane. He had been caught on the school grounds masturbating with a group of boys. This behavior was sufficiently bizarre to the school authorities for them to call in psychological help. Jimmy was the only boy who received the "help" since he was the only one in treatment before the incident. His psychologist, an upper-middle-class white woman, agreed that the behavior was insane and recommended his expulsion. No note was made of the fact that group masturbation with a prize to the first boy to ejaculate is not at all uncommon in certain subcultures. Jimmy was actually participating in a popular sport that was not at all strange or bizarre in his own culture. The other boys were admonished and then left alone.

In the medical model's attempts to get at the underlying cause of deviancy, a great deal of attention is paid to what the child does *wrong*. The child soon learns that the best way to get attention is to continue to do "wrong," even if the result is punishment. Behavioral psychologists define punishment empirically. Punishment is considered a response to a specific behavior, which, if given contingently to that behavior, will weaken the behavior. To many administrators and teachers, however, punishment is a procedure that *should* decrease the frequency of a particular behavior; but in reality, punishment thus regarded will often *increase* the behavior in question. Children learn that trips to the guidance counselor, the sessions of play therapy where juice and cookies are served, and time spent in the principal's office rather than in class, are the punishment-reward of misdeeds.

Another negative effect of the medical model is to transfer basic educational questions from the realm of education and place them in the hands of the "experts"— the psychologists and psychiatrists. When the school wants to suspend a child, they can refer him or her to a mental health expert who has the power to certify the child is "disturbed." The context of the behavior—including the possibility of teacher provocation—is ignored. And because psychiatric and psychological reports are treated as "confidential," in many cases there is no recourse to the resulting suspension; civil-liberties safeguards like hearings are usually bypassed.

The medical perspective toward the exceptional child can also lead to "administrative cures" where the child's behavior is "understood" through placing a diagnostic label on the child or perhaps through administratively placing him in a different program where different expectations can be held out for the child.

It is easy for a teacher to understand why a "dyslexic" or "brain-damaged" child does not learn to read. He does not learn to read because he is dyslexic or brain-damaged, but his failing to learn to read is what got him the label in the first place. Having a label placed on the child might help the teacher cope with his frustration, but it does not help the child to learn skills. Teachers should insist that every diagnosis be followed with two crucial questions: "So what?" and "What do I do now specifically?" The answers to such questions are far more helpful than labels.

Once a medically derived label is placed on the child there is little chance for escaping the special-education track. A self-fulfilling prophecy begins to take over, and escape from its effects can only be achieved if the parents move from the school district, place their child in a parochial or private school, or threaten the school administration through legal means. The status of "retarded" or "disturbed" can be lost only when the child drops out of school, is too old for the special-education program, or is expelled from the school system entirely.

On the other hand, a behavioral approach to exceptionality does not use diagnostic labels at all. The behavioral approach will instead carefully measure current levels of functioning and point to specific interventions that might or might not be helpful. Whether a particular method of reading or changing social behavior is effective is an empirical question, and behavior modification can provide the measurement system necessary to evaluate the intervention.

COMPULSORY EDUCATION AND DEVIANCY

Perhaps the greatest contribution to the problems of youth is the fact of universal and compulsory schooling. Not every child wants to, or can, attend school for the prolonged period of time required by law. If all adults in the United States were forced to become machinists or carpenters, we would experience an immediate and dramatic increase in work-related problems such as injuries, malingering, and so forth. Many physicians and lawyers would be abysmal failures as carpenters and would thus be considered deviant. This is analogous to what happens when we ask every child in the United States to become the same thing: a student. As long as law or custom compels more children to attend schools for longer and longer periods of time, studying a curriculum that is meaningless to them and under conditions that they find abhorrent, problems of "deviancy" will increase.

Certain kinds of deviancy have been theorized as directly related to the economy of a country and its gross national product. In subsistence economies it is unlikely that significant portions of the population will be regarded as too retarded or disturbed to work. Everyone is needed, and meaningful work—even if it is that of being a shepherd—can be found for all but the most grossly aberrant. In industrial economies, where profits are deemed more important than social welfare, a large proportion of the populace can be declared misfits, since such economies do not need so many workers.

There is no youth problem analogous to ours in less economically developed countries, such as Spain or Mexico. Although their schools are faced with many problems, they are not problems that require a large staff of attendance officers, guidance counselors, psychotherapists, correctional officers, and the like. As such

countries develop economically, more capital will be put
into their educational systems. If they follow the model of
the United States, insisting that every child between the
ages of six and sixteen attend school, they too will experience youth problems similar to ours.

SCHOOLS PRODUCE DEVIANTS

Less industrialized societies have had fewer deviants,
but most societies have had some. The most extreme
treatment of deviant children has been infanticide, which
was practiced by the Spartans and emulated as recently as
thirty years ago in Nazi Germany. In the Middle Ages
dwarfs and other deviants were treated as mild objects of
amusement, frequently performing the role of court
jester. The Church protected many deviants and was
instrumental in leading reforms in the treatment of them.

In America large institutions were built to house deviants and keep them from public view. In addition to the
penal institutions and hospitals that the state has erected
to protect society from the deviant, the military establishment has also been used. Very often the army serves as a
kind of home for the poor, and judges have often given
adolescents the Hobson's choice of entering a correctional
institution or joining the army. This serves the twofold
purpose of gaining control over the life of the deviant
and at the same time extending the power of the state by
filling the manpower needs of the military.

However, while thousands of deviants are still institutionalized, there has been a marked change in policies of
institutionalization. For example, only those perceived as
most severely afflicted are institutionalized for retardation, and thus the mean IQ of institutionalized patients
has dropped quite significantly. There has also been a
trend attempting to avoid incarceration of delinquents in

training schools, with more emphasis being placed on the use of smaller "halfway" houses. State hospitals have also become a little more reluctant to take children, although they have a well-documented tendency to assume that anyone referred to them must be mentally ill: since the behavior of many lower-class children is considered abnormal to white, middle-class medical staffs, the result is that minority-group children are more frequently admitted to institutions than their white counterparts. Some clinicians have even noted that many lower-class parents use the state hospitals as boarding schools, much in the same way that upper-class parents use residential private schools.

With the de-emphasis on institutionalization, the public school "special class" has become one of the most favored vehicles for handling deviant children or those children who "cannot profit from regular education procedures." In many ways special education has become a dumping ground for all the problems that school teachers and administrators do not want to face. Special education has been described by a prominent black educator, Dr. John Johnson, formerly an assistant superintendent of schools in Washington, D.C., as:

> part of the arrangement for cooling out students. It has helped to erect a parallel system which permits relief of institutional guilt and humiliation stemming from the failure to achieve competence and effectiveness in the task given to it by society. Special education is helping the regular school maintain its special programs (whether psychodynamic or behavior modification) for the "disruptive child" and the "slow learner," many of whom, for some strange reason, happen to be Black and poor and live in the inner city.

Psychotherapy and other forms of counseling are used extensively to treat deviants, and in many ways psy-

31243

chologists try to perform the function of protecting the deviant. But there is a fundamental difference between private practice and compulsory government-operated programs. In private psychiatric or psychological clinical practice, a voluntary arrangement is made between practitioner and patient. While the patient may not get his "money's worth" (most research indicates that children who receive psychotherapy get better at about the same rate as children who have essentially the same problems but do not receive psychotherapy), at least in most cases the arrangement is a voluntary one. In a school situation, however, the psychiatrist is paid by the state, decisions are made without consent of the children or their parents and sometimes even without a proper scientific rationale. For example, research is quite equivocal as to the benefits of special-class placement. Evidence exists that special-class placement results in stigmatizing children, and often they fall behind their matched counterparts in academic achievement.

ECONOMICS AND SPECIAL EDUCATION

Special education is big business. The United States Office of Education estimated that in 1972 over 1 million children were in special programs for the retarded, the disturbed, and the learning-disabled. In the latter part of 1973, Dr. Edwards Martin, associate commissioner of Education for the Handicapped, estimated that some 6 million children, approximately 10 percent of our school-aged population, suffered from some kind of handicapping condition, and some few millions more could profit from techniques developed in special education.

Special-education budgets run into the millions and millions of dollars. For example, in one typical community in California with a school population of 330,000, the total school budget is $240 million. More than 11 percent of this budget is spent for working with "deviant" students directly, and a considerably larger sum is expended when support services are included.

The percentage of the education budget spent for special education in urban areas is not qualitatively different. Merely to justify a payroll of such size, a large number of clients is needed.

The labeling process, as employed in our schools, is thus encouraged by economic factors. Special-education classes are expensive and require large staffs. These personnel need children to work with or they would not be needed by their school districts. Empty slots in such facilities must be filled to justify the program. How children get labeled becomes a matter of dollars and cents. If the state will reimburse the school district for every "emotionally disturbed" child, but will not provide additional services or funding for the mentally retarded, there occurs a subtle and perhaps unconscious pressure to have children labeled as emotionally disturbed rather than mentally retarded. Legislatures do not disburse money to help children in general but earmark both money and services for particular *kinds* of children; categories are usually designated, such as that of emotionally disturbed children, or of children with specific learning disabilities. Then it is the responsibility of the administrators to see that their districts receive as much money as possible, so that the burden will not fall on local property owners—a burden that might endanger the livelihood of the administrator. Thus good administrators will keep ears tuned toward whispers of where the government is willing to spend money. Once the financing is obtained for specific learning disabilities, let us say, then the district finds the population to fill that category. There are few occasions when a school district fails to locate the child population required for funding.

Schools should not be provided with financial incentives to find exceptional children. They should be provided with adequate money to do their job properly, and the payoff should be placed on reducing deviancy, not merely labeling it.

THE STRUCTURE OF PRODUCING DEVIANCE

Schools operate to produce deviance in other ways than by having inflexible structures and rigid rules, or by predefining who is to learn what and at what rate. They also produce deviance by their very size and structure. Ecological psychologists have investigated the degree to which structures (which they would call behavior settings) influence behavior. Their findings have important implications for schools. Barker and Gump found that population density has a profound effect not only on behavior but also on the way that behavior is perceived. One discovery was that students in small schools participate in a wider variety of extracurricular activities than do students in large schools. A considerably larger proportion of small-school students will hold positions of importance and responsibility and derive more satisfaction from their school experience than will students in large schools. Thus small-school students are more readily socialized to the prevailing group norms, and a more narrow range of social behavior is found.

This also has a great effect on marginal students. Where the school is underpopulated, the efforts and initiative of marginal students are appreciated by the majority, with the result that marginal students are almost forced to hold positions of responsibility, and learn a great many social skills, which are reinforced by the general school population. In larger schools, the more marginal student feels like an outsider and does not feel forced in any way to participate in a positive manner in school activities. The fact of life for the marginal student in a large school is that he is only a number. The larger the school, the easier it becomes to exclude the outsider, or the one who is different in any respect. That is one of the reasons for the high dropout rate in urban high schools.

As size increases, voluntary participation decreases—students become observers of events rather than actual participants. For example, there are still only eleven men on a football team, and because of the competition, the chances of playing varsity sports are considerably smaller in a large school. The rest of the students must make up the audience. If resistance to nonparticipation exists, school authorities will increase coercion. The more that resistance is manifested, the more the resisters will be labeled as deviant, delinquent, or emotionally disturbed.

Social class, ethnic background, and the numbers of children that will get into trouble with authority can virtually be predicted by knowing the number of square feet in a school building and the number of students per square foot. Rules are a reflection of the size of schools, and deviancy is a reflection of rules.

The school is a territory inhabited by groups, and a territory that will be staked out and defended against intruders. The school, like any organism, will try to propagate itself and its rituals and rites. Those in charge of the school's survival and perpetuation monitor the behavior of group members for evidence of behaviors that might destroy or disrupt the life patterns of the territory.

The label "deviancy" is usually applied to any members who threaten the niche that the schools occupy in our society. Primarily, but not always, children who have been so labeled become the waste products of our school system. This is done at a considerable cost to our society, both in the maintenance of these children in the deviant status, and in their future behavior when they fail to learn the skills necessary to become productive members of our society.

2

Children Can Change Schools

Technology in the form of behavior modification can help the child who is perceived as deviant. It can directly change his environment, including those key people who control his life. Currently, establishment-oriented groups —administrators, teachers, and high-status children— retain control over the power structure within schools. A study undertaken in a California school district has, however, demonstrated that this control may be neutralized, or even turned to positive effect, by developing the capacity of children to change the behaviors of those establishment-oriented groups that want to change the subject children. The experiments reported by this study employed the methodologies inherent in an ecological approach to descriptions of behavior—the use of "goodness of fit" models of behavior rather than medical models or social deviancy models. Although in this study the experimenters worked with pupils labeled as deviant, the results suggest the possibilities for application of these methods to whole student populations—normals and deviants alike—who suffer from the present uses of power within our school system.

The four experiments described by this study involved four potentials of the ecosystem found to exist in schools: changing teacher tolerance of noise, changing of behavior of a normal child by children labeled as deviant or special, changing the perceptions of normals toward the settings to which the "special-education" children had been assigned, and the modification of teacher behavior by students who had been labeled as deviant or special.

The experiments took place in a rural community in California. Anglos comprised the predominant group in the school system; there was also a large Chicano population, and a small black community. Each experiment describes a special application of the ecological-behavioral approach and is reported here as representative of that methodology.

CHANGING TOLERANCE FOR NOISE

One of the basic issues of teacher-pupil interaction is the complaint that children are too noisy. Rather than making an attempt to eliminate the noise problem by producing more quiet children, the approach taken in this experiment was intended to promote teacher readiness to accept the children's spontaneous noise level.

The four classrooms chosen for this experiment were highly controlled by the teachers in charge. None of the four teachers involved was likely to prefer an increase of classroom noise level, since all four had received considerable recognition for skill in modifying the behavior of deviant children and maintaining quiet, closely structured classrooms. One of the four, Ann Watson, had been the first teacher in the district to develop a program that used operant conditioning or Skinnerian teaching principles, and had been a consultant to various districts throughout the state in training new special-education teachers to use Skinner-derived programs, for which she had received significant professional recognition. Ann had taught the sixth grade at Orange School in California for twelve years and had instituted a token economy in her sixth-grade classroom in the late fifties. It was one of the first token-economy systems developed in a regular classroom in the United States. She was a capable teacher in her use of the token-economy system and positive reinforcement. The class was well run, with few behavior problems. Ann had spent several years without having to refer a single child to the office or to the parents for correction. Later on, she had developed precision teaching techniques in reading and math. In addition, she had developed her own system of behavioral objectives, which were written prescriptively for each child in each academic program. Ann was considered by all observers to be an outstanding teacher. Her classroom was one of the best organized— but also one of the quietest in the school. Over the twelve years that she had been using behavior modification, Ann Watson had very slowly developed her class into one where there was little interaction between student and student, and student and teacher. Most of the classroom work consisted of ditto sheets, task sheets, or other forms of individualized work. The students were learning very effectively, but there was little social interaction between the children in the classroom. The token-economy system and Ann's positive reinforcement were used to develop a quiet and submissive class of students. The children completed assignments, but there was little evidence of joy or pleasure about their learning. The students were placed in traditional rows and most classwork was done by each child individually at his own desk. The token-economy system paid the largest number of rewards for working quietly, hand-raising, and following directions. The class had become one of quiet, submissive children.

As part of the experiment, audio tapes made on recorders hidden in these classrooms measured the noise level. The tapes were replayed into a decibel counter and the five highest readings were averaged. The first of five weeks during which the experiment was conducted was used as a baseline week, and statistical techniques were used to measure changes. After the baseline readings had been made, the special-education supervisor praised each teacher generally for competence and specifically for tolerance of noise and freedom of self-expression allowed the children. The supervisor then asked each teacher's permission to use his or her classroom as a model, stating the purpose was to provide opportunities for other teachers to observe how much freedom of self-expression and freedom of behavior a good teacher allowed students. Visitors, including the superintendent of the district, were brought into the classrooms during the succeeding four weeks, and the students' freedom of self-expression and behavior were underscored by the supervisor (in the presence of these visitors and the teacher) as being worthy of emulation.

Not only was there a dramatic change in the level of noise in all four classrooms, but the classroom activity did become freer. Students were now allowed to leave their seats without asking permission, to sharpen pencils, talk with peers, or go to the bathroom. The children also worked in groups rather than spending the day in isolation at their own desks.

The experiment demonstrated that teachers can

change quite radically in the face of rewards such as praise, reinforcement, and modeling. In this case, observers of high prestige—supervisors and superintendents—were bestowers of such rewards by communicating their sense of the good job the teachers were doing. That is, the positive aspects of the teachers' performance became the underlined focus, rather than assumptions of "obsoleteness," "rigidity," and "maintenance of the status quo," which are usually communicated to teachers by reform-minded people who enter schools in an attempt to introduce innovative programs. Thus, instead of encountering teacher resistance to change, this experiment resulted in indications of the potential for effective change.

DEVIANT CHILDREN CHANGE NORMALS

Another experiment consisted of training special-education children (officially designated as emotionally handicapped) to modify the behavior of normal children. The normal children were observed to scapegoat the special-education children, using derogatory terms such as "retards" and "rejects from the funny farm." "Saluggi," in which bigger children would throw one child's cap around while the unfortunate owner ran from one to another in a vain attempt to reclaim his property, was a favorite game for the normals. Being teased, ignored, and ridiculed were parts of the social role thrust upon the special-education children.

Work with the special-education children consisted of two resource teachers providing individual counseling, made up of one thirty-minute session per week over a period of nine weeks, during which behavior-modification principles were explicitly explained and illustrated to the children.

The special-education children were asked to list those children they wished to spend more time with, and to describe specifically the behavior of the children whose behavior they wanted to change.

Among the things counted were the number of hostile physical contacts that took place on the playground and the number of snubs or hostile remarks directed toward each child. Positive contacts with particular children were recorded if the special-education child's goal was to increase such interactions. The data collection was done by the special-education children and handed in each day to their counselors. Their observations were corroborated by independent observers.

The pupil behavioral engineers were taught several educational methods taken from reinforcement theory: (1) Extinction: walking away from the chase-the-cap game, breaking eye contact with the provocative children, and ignoring negative remarks (the children received primary reinforcers such as candy from their counselor for each instance in which they succeeded). (2) Reinforcement: explicitly sharing toys or candy or giving compliments to those children who made positive contact with the behavior engineers. (3) Incompatible responses: reinforcing children to participate in activities such as running games with which negative behaviors were incompatible. (4) Setting contingencies: helping other children with homework, crafts, and school activities, and so forth.

Observers in this peer-to-peer experiment unobstrusively checked and recorded positive and negative comments by the "clients" of the special-education children. From the data thus obtained it was noted that the student behavior engineers were able to manage a fairly subtle posture, which perhaps can best be illustrated by a description of a typical reaction of one child to her experience as a participant in this study. For the purposes of making this description, let's call her Sarah.

Sarah was, admittedly, one of the most successful examples in the peer-to-peer behavior-modification project. She was a sixth-grade student, very pretty—auburn hair, a little upturned nose with freckles—and to adults the picture of an extremely attractive, vivacious, and intelligent little girl. Yet she had equally extreme behavioral problems in the classroom and on the playground at school with both peers and teachers. While a gifted student, Sarah had never received a report card with even average grades. She was in a classroom of four teachers and approximately 120 students and was perceived as a troublemaker by most of the students and teachers who knew her. As a result, perhaps, Sarah made frequent visits to the administrative office and was therefore equally and similarly known by the secretaries, the principal, and the vice-principal. In spite of her attractiveness and intelligence she was not liked by fellow students. Sarah also appeared to be a very unhappy person, perhaps partly because she had tried very hard to be friends with some of the boys and girls who shared her classroom, and had not succeeded.

After exposure to the program described here, however, Sarah changed within six months to a student with a B average, who had not been referred to the administrative staff in the last four of six months, and who had a wide group of friends. (She had been invited to three birthday parties, had had moviegoing invitations from two students, fourteen invitations to go swimming at other children's homes, plus invitations to two slumber parties, and sixty-five invitations to visit a friend's home after school.)

Teachers made such comments about Sarah (after her enrollment in this project) as: "I can't imagine what's happened to her, but whatever it is, it's wonderful"; "she used to be constantly fighting with me, the other teachers, and the students, but now she's charming and delightful;

she's now one of the most popular students in the room";
"I don't know what happened to Sarah, but it's great"; "it
was always obvious that Sarah was intelligent, but it was
even more obvious that she never used any of it"; and "all
of us are pleased with Sarah."

When Sarah was asked about what the project had
meant to her, including the details of gathering the data
and handing it in and learning specific interventions with
peers, she gave the following interview:

"I didn't get along with most of the kids very well
back then, so he [Mr. Fabraconti] asked me if I would like
to be in the program with him. At first I didn't know, but
then I thought I might as well try it; at least I would get
out of the classroom for part of the time.

"One of the first things that I did was try to change a
person's attitude against me. Mr. Fabraconti asked me to
name three people that I wanted to make friends with.
They were Raphael, Jim, and Amy. Then the next thing
he said was how many times did any of them say nice
things about me. And he wanted me to carry a little card
around with me and mark it down on the card. So I
carried the cards around with me in my purse and I
marked down on the card every time the guys said anything nice to me. Then I'd sit down with Mr. Fabraconti
and we'd talk about it. After two weeks we talked about
how many times we could increase the nice things they
said to me.

"We used a theory that every time Amy said something nice, I'd offer to help her with her work, or something similar to that. Or, if Amy complimented me on
something, I'd compliment her back. Then for the first
two weeks I ignored her if she said anything bad to me.
But then, when she said anything nice to me, I'd help her
with her work, or I sat down and asked her to do something with me, or something like that. That's the way it
went pretty much.

"With Jim, he was the one that was always saying bad things about me. And for the first three weeks when he said something bad, I would just ignore him; I'd turn my back on him, like he hadn't said anything, or something like that. Then when we sat down with Mr. Fabraconti again, and he asked me if I could think of anything to improve it with Jim so that he would quit saying bad things about me, I said, 'Well, I think if I keep ignoring him, it's going to be okay, because he doesn't say as many bad things about me anymore.'

"The first time that Jim ever said anything to me that was even nice, like even hello, or the first time he even walked by me without saying something bad to me, I gave him a great big smile and I said, 'Hi, Jim, how are you today?' When I first did that, Jim looked like he was going to die. Because I guess I had never said anything nice to him before and you could see that Jim didn't know what to do with it when I said, 'Hi, Jim, how are you today?' He was so surprised his mouth just opened and he looked at me and he couldn't think of anything to say. It took him by surprise so much that he didn't say anything bad to me for about four days. The first time I had a chance I said to him, 'Hi, Jim, what are you doing?' And he was by himself then, and I was with a group of other kids and I asked him if he would like to come over and talk with us for a while. Jim was so surprised again he didn't know what to do, and he came over and talked with us and I smiled at him as nice as I could, and boy, I'll tell you the count on him really went down. He wasn't calling me any names at all. That's all it took with Jim, I just ignored him for a while and then I was real friendly to him when he was nice to me and he's always nice to me now. . . .

"Then with Raphael it was the same thing. It was how many times he would call me names. Raphael was always calling me names; in fact, Raphael calls everybody names. I don't think anybody likes Raphael. I'd write down every time Raphael called me a name and I'd put it on the card, and every day after school I'd take the cards into Mrs. Christenson, the school secretary, and give them to her.

"Then when I'd sat down with Mr. Fabraconti and talked to him again, we'd talk about all of the stuff we'd written down on the cards and how that was helping me and how it was going and everything. But Raphael was really a tough one. He'd always call me names when all of his friends were around and they would all laugh at me and so would he and he would just keep on doing it. They all thought it was really funny. So what I did, every time he called me a name I just ignored him. But sometimes with Raphael, ignoring him didn't work because the other kids laughed and made Raphael want to do it more. The next thing I did was I would turn away and I wouldn't even look at him. I did with Raphael just like I did with Jim, but with Raphael I saw that if he was standing around with his friends I tried to stay away from him, because if he had some kids around that would laugh, he would always like to call you names so he could get the attention of the kids. So I knew with Raphael, if he had a bunch of other kids standing around, you had to stay away from him because he was going to call you names. But I waited until Raphael was by himself and I walked up to him and I'd say, 'Hi, Raphael, how are you today?' and I'd smile at him and he was just like Jim, he just didn't know what to do.

"The first time, though, with Raphael, when I said, 'Hi, how are you?' he still called me a name, because he thought I was being mean to him, because I'd never said anything nice to Raphael and really, hardly anybody ever does. I guess the only way Raphael ever gets anybody's attention is by calling people names and being mean and fighting. But after six or seven times, when Raphael was by himself, I'd say, 'Hi, Raphael, how are you today?' he'd kind of smile a little bit and I smiled right back at him. Then one time I was standing with a bunch of my friends again and Raphael came by all by himself. It used to be that anytime I was with any of my friends and Raphael came by—by himself—I'd call him names and poke fun at him and say, 'Look at him with his curly head, look at the little boy.' Raphael isn't really very big for a sixth-grader, he's smaller than the rest of the kids and he's very self-conscious about this. So when Raphael came by and saw me with my friends, I think he thought I was going to tease him, but I said, 'Hi, Raphael, how are you?' and one of the other girls said it too, and then we started talking to him and he came over and talked to us for a while, and then we were going to go play a game we called Nation Ball and we asked him to come along and play with us and I smiled at him and he came over with us and he smiled back and he played with us.

"Then another time I was playing basketball and I asked Raphael if he would like to play basketball and he did play with us, and every time he did something good in basketball I said, 'Hey, Raphael, that was great,' or something nice to him, and he really liked this, you could tell. After we played basketball, he didn't call me names anymore and I just kept being friendly to him and smiling every time he came by.

"I think next year when I go to junior high school in the seventh grade that if I don't get along with the kids very well, I'll need this and it's going to help me and I know how to use it and I know I'll need this theory like Mr. Fabraconti taught me to do. I don't think I'd use the card to mark things down anymore, I don't think I need it anymore, I can handle it on my own by just ignoring kids, saying nice things to them, or asking them to do nice things with me that are fun, or helping them with their homework. I really liked knowing how I can make kids like me, or make kids leave me alone. I never knew how to do that before, and that's really been great, I really liked that."

While Sarah may have been exceptional in terms of this experiment, conclusions from the data showed generally that deviant children could change the behaviors of normal children, and that hostile physical contacts or instances of teasing and so on were considerably reduced as a result of the program. Moreover, approach behaviors such as invitations to parties and invitations to join in play were considerably accelerated. At no time during the course of the experiment did any teacher intervene with the normal children and encourage or limit their behavior.

Behavior modification, then, appears to be a powerful tool that can give deviant children the social skills and power to change the behavior of others toward them. While the deviant children undoubtedly changed their own behavior as well, the important thing remains that they dramatically changed the behavior of others toward them.

CHANGING THE PERCEPTIONS OF NORMALS TOWARD SPECIAL-EDUCATION SETTINGS

These experiments included not only inspection and observation of the contacts between participants in the school setting but also the study of contacts between participants and the setting itself. The experimenters took the view that the exclusion of special-education children from the physical surroundings in which the normal children experienced school was significant in terms of loss of prestige and concomitant harassment that the deviants were sometimes subjected to. For years special educators have recognized that the normal child shuns contact with the special child—avoiding going into or near the special-education classroom, perhaps for fear of being similarly labeled. As a result of this, placement in a special class for the emotionally disturbed or retarded may well become another self-fulfilling prophecy.

An attempt was made to change the perception of normal children toward the special-education classroom. The experimenters decided to make the special class a place that students would want to get into, not out of. The goal was to make the program so interesting and exciting to students that there would actually be a waiting list to get into the class. To do this it was decided to have the class participate in exciting activities that would attract the regular students. The first activity selected was a wrestling program led by the special-class teacher and his aide. The teacher arranged to get wrestling mats from the high schools three days a week. He took the mats out on the lawn in plain view of the regular classes and taught his students how to wrestle. They made sure that this always started just before recess, so that the wrestling program overlapped recess a few moments and allowed the regular-class students the opportunity to see the teacher instructing the boys. The regular students became quite interested in wrestling and there was soon a clamor from them to get into wrestling.

Each special-education student was given permission to select a friend and invite him into the wrestling class. This was worked out with the regular teacher so that students in the regular class were released from class time to go to the special class for wrestling. The wrestling class was then moved into the special classroom itself. This helped to make the special classroom a desirable place. The special-class students controlled the access to the program and would only invite students who had been nice to them.

In addition to wrestling, the teacher developed boxing, ceramics, and an arts and crafts program. With the additional funds that special education received, he bought a kiln, molds, and materials for his program. The procedure followed was the same. The special-class students invited others to participate in the arts and crafts program in the special class. After two school months, the biggest problem with the special class was the waiting list and the requests for admittance to the class. The teacher also participated in afterschool sports and was seen frequently on the playground and in regular classes. The special-class teacher was accepted as one of the staff by students and teachers. The class took a number of exciting field trips as well, including a fishing trip. They also sponsored a chess tournament in the special class, with prizes going to the winners.

In November the special-class program started an ice-skating class. Ice time, skates, and an instructor were purchased by the special-education department, and the entire special class went ice-skating three times a week. The special class invited selected students from the regular class to go ice-skating with them. On three different occasions they even invited an entire regular class to go ice-skating. Very rapidly, regular-class students were flocking to the special class to see what exciting things were going on. The special-class teacher kept a count of the number of visitors from regular class to the special-education classroom. There was an increase of over 900 percent in the number of visitors to the class. In addition, more than six teachers out of a staff of twenty-two wanted to become a part of the special-education staff.

TEACHER BEHAVIOR AS MODIFIED
BY CHILDREN

A seventh- and eighth-grade junior high school was selected for studying modification of teacher behavior by children, largely because it had been found to be the most difficult school in the district for reintegrating special-education students into regular classes. At the time the project was undertaken, this school had earned a reputation for having a large number of older teachers very hostile to minority groups and especially to those who had been labeled "exceptional."

As a result, the school under study had more special-education classes and a higher proportion of children in special education than any school in the district. The school, with approximately 650 students, had five special classes for problem children, each class numbering fifteen. This meant that 10 percent of students attending the school had been placed in classes for students with behavioral problems. Both administrative fiat and personal consultation with teachers had failed to change this scenario in any way. In consequence, it was decided that only the children themselves could be taught to teach teachers' behaviors.

Seven children from one special-education class, whose ages ranged from twelve to fifteen years, were selected by the experimenters to be instructed as behavior engineers. All of the seven had been labeled as incorrigible by a number of social agencies working in the community: the police department, school officials, probation officers, etc. In a class day organized into seven forty-three-minute periods, these seven children met with a special-class teacher for three of those periods and were integrated into regular classes during four periods.

Instruction and practice in behavior-modification

theory and techniques were given by special-class teachers during one period each day. Techniques taught and practiced during these classes included such things as establishing eye contact with teachers, asking for extra help with lessons, sitting straight, nodding in agreement while teachers spoke, and using reinforcing comments like "Gee, it makes me feel good and work so much better when you teach the lesson that way." The techniques and phrases were taught to be used contingently with teacher performance, but any judgment of that performance—whether positive or negative toward the child—was left to the child.

Pupils were also taught to break eye contact with teachers when receiving a scolding, to ignore teachers' provocations, and to practice the "Ah hah" reaction—a technique of first understanding an explanation, then asking for a repetition of the explanation, and then interrupting the second explanation by exclaiming, "Ah hah, now I understand!" These techniques were explicitly taught to the children and were practiced repeatedly, using simulation, role-playing, and videotapes to allow the children to monitor both their own and others' performances, so that, under both class and teacher promptings, factors that seemed targets for change could be adjusted. Attempts were made to use these procedures with and without the children counting. The projects were considerably more successful when the children took data.

One of the behavior engineers chosen for the project was Joseph. Joseph was typical of a student labeled incorrigible—five feet ten inches, black, weighing 185 pounds when he was fourteen years old, and still in the eighth grade. Joseph had been kept in school because of his outstanding athletic ability in football, basketball, baseball, and wrestling. He was known among his peers and the adult members of the community where he lived as one of the toughest kids in town. Even students as much as three years older than he were frightened of him because of his great strength combined with viciousness. Joseph in a fight was the sort for whom no holds were barred: he would kick, claw, bite, elbow, knee, or use any object he could lay his hands on. He had knocked students unconscious with bottles, sticks, and chairs. He was so strong that when the junior high school wrestling team met other junior high schools as opponents, a high school opponent was selected for Joseph.

Joseph had been in trouble since the first grade. He had a long history of talking back to teachers, using profanity, fighting with students, and occasionally striking teachers or school principals. Hc had been expelled for one forty-day period because he had struck a principal with a stick. Frequently he had been sent home by teachers, teacher aides, and the school principal for direct disobedience and defiance. He had been arrested when he was twelve and had been on probation for two and one-half years prior to his placement in the special class.

The staff of the junior high school assumed that Joseph would go directly from the special class at junior high school to continuation high school. Continuation high schools in California are operated on separate campuses, and there is no integration of the students. In this particular district, very few students ever return to regular school from continuation school. In continuation school the students attend for only 180 minutes per day and spend the rest of the time loose in the community.

A specific technique that was most helpful to Joseph was to learn how to make small talk with the teacher. The special-classroom teacher worked with Joseph and encouraged him to stay after class or to be early for class and talk with the teacher. Joseph soon found, much to his great surprise, that most of the teachers were aware of his athletic ability and were most eager to talk to him about the recent games he had played in. Joseph soon developed into an expert at what he called "chat with the teachers." He became quite friendly with the teachers, and the special-class teacher soon heard numerous comments like "I don't know what you've done with Joseph, but it's fantastic!"; "Joseph is a different boy than he ever was before"; "I think Joseph is one of the greatest kids in school now"; "What did you do to make Joseph so friendly?" Joseph very quickly switched from being perceived as one of the worst-behaved boys in the school to being one of the students best liked by peers and teachers.

Videotaping proved extremely effective in one intervention used by Joseph. He had never learned how to smile. When he thought he was smiling, he was actually using a menacing leer that was quite frightening to peers, as well as to teachers. Joseph used the leer when he wanted to please an adult or a student, apparently unaware of the effect of his facial expression. When Joseph was asked to smile while being videotaped, he gave his usual ferocious leer, and this was played back for him. Joseph was stunned at seeing his frightening smile. The others in the class teased Joseph and laughed about his smile when they saw it on videotape. Then they all told him—as did the teacher—that this smile was indeed frightening to them. Eventually Joseph did learn how to use a very charming and disarming smile whenever teachers directed positive behavior toward him.

Not only were Joseph and his co-behavior engineers transformed into some of the best-liked, most highly respected students in the school but the special-class teacher as well received a great deal of praise for the remarkable changes in the students. This particular group of students and the teacher became somewhat of a folk legend within the junior high school. Even the most difficult "old-timer" teachers were quite startled and pleased by the progress of the students. The special-class teacher had been a new teacher to the school, and the experienced staff at the school were impressed by his ability to change the students and deal with such a difficult group of kids.

The students were integrated into math, social studies, homemaking, English, shop, physical education, and art, and they used these techniques in all of these classes. The regular-class teachers were both male and female and had from two to twenty-seven years of teaching experience. The students were successful in changing all of their teachers, regardless of their age, sex, experience, or subject taught—with the exception of physical education, a class that students and the special-class teacher decided was different, in that it was extremely large.

In the project, students handed in their data daily to the special-class teacher, receiving points for doing so. In addition, the teacher graphed both the negative and positive comments and kept these records of the project posted in the room. The students were quite pleased with the charts and felt that they could see the success of their particular phase of the program much better when it was displayed upon graph paper. The teacher would discuss the project and its particular phases with the entire group. They took great pride in their project and the success they were having with teachers. The results indicated that all the students were able to modify teacher behavior, at least temporarily. Statistical tests indicated that such changes were not due to chance, and the children reported feelings of success in changing the behavior of the target teachers. The students had started out being integrated into regular classes for only one class during the day, but as the project proceeded, many of the students were integrated for four such periods. By the end of the project all students were attending school for the entire day, remaining in the special class for three periods and spending the other four periods in regular classes. None of them had to be sent on to the continuation high school.

The target teachers were quite dependent upon the reinforcement schedule of the students. During the last phase of the project, when students went on an extinction phase and stopped all positive contacts, there was a significant drop-off in positive teacher behavior. After the completion of the project, when the students reinstituted positive reinforcements, the teachers' positive behavior also increased. Students were able, in many cases, to extinguish negative contacts with teachers completely. This is extremely significant since, before the project, almost the only contact these students had with teachers was negative. The students in the project did feel that they had more power over teachers and their environment than they ever had before.

THE POSSIBILITIES FOR CHANGE

The success of these experiments indicates that behavior-modification technology can be used in many ways, not simply in unexciting fashions. Given an ecological approach, behavior modification has intriguing possibilities for application to schools. While such a technology has ordinarily been used only by established groups, this does not have to be the case. Children can use it as well as teachers; teachers can use it as well as administrators; parents can apply it to their children, but children can and do apply it to their parents. The possibilities and permutations of its application may well be infinite, and behavior modification can help reduce the coercion that is such an integral part of today's schools.

The coercion involved in the process of American education is among the most significant reasons for the present breakdown in that system. We do not mean by this to designate only compulsory-attendance laws as having been responsible for the failures of such a system, but, as well, the ensuing fact that all authority—in most classrooms, at least—rests with the teacher. We find little room for autonomous action on the part of the pupil, even in such basic areas as scholarship.

Many scholars have documented the observation that teachers discourage all but *the* correct answer, and that students frequently must "psych out" their teachers in order to get credit for their work. The patience and goodwill of some teachers may keep classrooms functioning as a system of benevolent dictatorship; but when patience and goodwill are not present in the classroom, it soon functions as a system of outright dictatorship wherein all direction is given by the teacher and all actions are prescribed, with deviations from such prescriptions severely punished. As a result, much behavioral research has begun to be concentrated on the effects of self-control, which appear to be superior to those of systems in which control is rigidly maintained in the hands of the teacher.

One of the important elements in the experiments described here appeared to be the use of videotapes and observers. Once objectives were set and goals agreed upon, the objectivity enforced on the situation by the use of observers and by the mechanical tools used in the instruction helped to document what was actually happening and how well the goals agreed upon were being met. The use of such methods, in addition to providing a teaching orientation, also provided an entirely new area of study for both students and teachers. The work accomplished in such courses of study was shown to be susceptible to replication and refinement. Because of its technological components, not only teaching but the learning process itself can become more efficient and rewarding.

Behavior modification, like any other technology, can be used for good and for bad, for helping people win their rights or for taking their rights away from them, for teaching them or maltreating them. The real question is how it will be used and by whom. All parties involved in the pursuit of education, *including* children as well as those in power, have to be more explicit about their goals, and then they can change the schools. They can use technology as one of their major allies in reaching their goals, or they can pretend technology does not exist.

3

Behavioral Approaches at Work

SETTING BEHAVIORAL GOALS

Many behavioral psychologists believe a major problem in schools is that neither goals nor methods are made clear either within the individual classroom or within the school system as a whole. Parents are asked to surrender their children for twelve years with a vague promise that in the end they will be properly socialized, knowledgeable, and ready to function in the adult world. Nor are children consulted about the goals they are expected to reach or the methods that will be employed to help them reach these goals. As children grow older, they have more and more definite ideas on what is important to them and they want a voice in deciding how they will spend their time. Hence there is often a sharp conflict over what transpires in the classroom.

The problem lies, in part, with teachers expecting or being pressured to "cover the curriculum," regardless of its applicability or learner motivation. Another aspect of this problem is that many goals sound good rhetorically but are impossible to define.

One classic example is the teacher who sets the goal that his class should be "creative"; to bring this about he will "work with each child to the limits of his capacity." Close examination of his statement leaves the parent, administrator, or child with the uneasy feeling that "creative" is so subjective that virtually *any* activity could apply. The teacher would have an almost impossible task trying to reinforce creative behavior, without criteria by which to judge whether a child was learning to be creative or not.

Similarly, the word *capacity* is used in such a way that it cannot be defined or analyzed. Scholars, philosophers, and psychometricians cannot define *capacity* in any satisfactory way. How does the teacher expect to do so?

The teacher should state exactly how he means the word if his success is to be judged intelligently, and if the administrator, parent, or child is to decide to have any part of his program.

We all have the capacity to be thieves and liars, but it is doubtful that the teacher had this in mind when he asked the children to work to their "capacity." Besides, who is to judge what are the capacities of the children? Should it be the children themselves, their parents, the school administrator? Or would it be left up to the sole discretion of the teacher? And what will he use for evidence?

Examples of other subjective criteria are "to understand the principles of science," "to appreciate literature," or "to learn reading or mathematics skills." The problem with goals that are couched in terms like "to learn," "to know," "to appreciate," or "to understand" is that they refer to internal processes that can only be inferred.

These goals do not state how we can know whether a subject matter is "appreciated." What *kind* of literature does the teacher want the child to appreciate? Will pornographic literature meet the criterion? Probably not, but who is to know?

The best way to avoid vagueness within the classroom is to reinforce teachers for stating goals behaviorally, and then to reinforce them even more for reaching these goals within specified time limits. To state a goal behaviorally is to state explicitly what the learner will have to do in order to demonstrate that he has achieved the goal that was specified.

Behavioral goals are most often used by teachers, but there is no reason why they cannot be used by pupils as well. Administrators can use behavioral goals, and so can parents. In all cases, they must be made explicit. The behavior displayed by teacher or child, administrator or parent has to be overt, unambiguous, and specific. Only observable acts or products should be the focus of reinforcement.

Statements of behavioral objectives should use terms such as "to identify," "to list," "to describe," "to translate," or "to demonstrate." Phrases such as "to answer a specific number of questions at a specific rate" are also acceptable behavioral goals, since the criteria are clear-cut.

Some people argue that behavioral objectives can only be used with subject matter like mathematics. They can, however, be used with complex social behavior, as well as with subjects such as literature and creative writing.

For example, many teachers are concerned that their pupils develop into "responsible citizens." Using the behavioral method, the teacher would first ask, "What exactly is a responsible citizen (or how do I know it when I see it?) and what behavior does that entail?" The second question would be "How will anyone know when this objective has been reached?"

"Responsible citizenship" would have to be translated into its behavioral components. This might mean having students evolve an orderly and fair system of working together. The specific problems of the class might include lining up for dismissal, or the elimination of scapegoating of particular class members.

For the first problem area, the teacher's objectives might include "Lining up at the door according to a prearranged plan so that every child has an opportunity to be first." If the objective is decided on by the class, and if consequences are clearly stated, the class can reinforce behavior that makes sharing and cooperating easier. The children are developing "responsible citizenship," but they are also working with specific curricula and objectives.

In order to handle the problem of scapegoating, the behavioral objectives can include "to praise all classmates for appropriate behavior, and to include everyone in all games and activities." The teacher and the children have the opportunity to arrange events that will facilitate cooperation in this way. The children (and the teacher, too) can be reinforced for particular behaviors, or approximations, that the class wants used.

Similarly, specific teaching plans can be developed for cognitive development and scholarship. Rather than trying to "teach children how to think," behavioral objectives and curricula can be written "to have children differentiate among statements that are (a) factual, (b) based upon inference, and (c) statements of values."

When objectives are stated in such terms, specific behaviors to be developed and curriculum materials will follow naturally. Lists of statements containing values, inferences, and statements of fact can be written. Pupils can be taught to differentiate among the three by analyzing stories, newscasts, films, and related materials. Students can learn which kind of statement is appropriate for what kind of use, and can be reinforced for that appropriate use.

"Learning how to read" can be translated into behavioral objectives such as "answering specific questions about the main idea presented in specific books." The more specific the objective, the easier it will be to teach and reach.

Setting behavioral objectives does not have to mean filling in the blanks in programmed texts. Teaching children convergent thinking is not enough in our complex society. They must also learn how to make inferences and how to solve problems. These objectives, too, can be translated into behavioral terms. They can be written in the following manner: "Given such and such a problem, the student will list ten ways to solve the problem." Again, criteria for success and conditions under which the student will demonstrate his skills must be specified.

Complex curriculum areas, such as creative writing and fine arts, can also be taught through a combination of establishing behavioral objectives and reinforcing specific behaviors. For example, one teacher of an inner-city class wanted to improve the children's writing skills and the quality of stories written in her class. She had tried to foster creative writing by showing the class interesting pictures that they could respond to in writing. She told exciting stories herself and encouraged the children to make up their own endings. She also attempted to create an open and free atmosphere in the classroom. Her tactics were unsuccessful. The children seldom wrote anything. When they did write, the stories tended to be short (six to ten sentences in a fifth-grade class) and were dull and repetitive.

A sample of the students' work follows. The stories were written under conditions of inspiration, without any more specific objectives than the attempt to improve the quality of writing and the fostering of creativity. What follows is writing directly transcribed from the class and representative of the class work:

STUDENT A: I like to play football. Sometimes I like to play baseball. Sometimes I go to the boys Club. because we can play pool, hockey, basketball, swimming, Gym.

STUDENT B: I like to play football with my friend I like to go swimming in the boys school

STUDENT C: I like to go swimming. I like to rid Bikes. I like to run all day. I like to play games. Jailbreak pull off. roundup tag. freeze tag Pull of is my favorite games.

With the same students, the teacher changed her teaching procedures to behavioral methods. She shifted her goal from "to teach children to be creative" to "to teach children to increase the number of words in stories." A number of more complex objectives, which included "using different words in stories," "using new words," and "increasing the number of ideas presented in stories," were also set.

The teacher reinforced, through a token system, successful mastery of skills. Besides the quantitative improvements in the stories, independent raters, ignorant of the teaching methods used, judged the stories written under the specific curriculum-reinforcement procedure as superior to those written under conditions of inspiration.

Some of the stories written under the specific curriculum-reinforcement conditions follow. Again, the stories are directly transcribed and are representative of all the students' writing.

"My Classroom" In mi class we have Arts and Craft. We make molds, beans, flower, houses out of sticks, pictures, Art, painting. We move the board. We have licks on our doors and cabinet. We have lots, and lots of things. We go on trips. We went to the Planetarium, and the Museum of Natural History and the Bronx Zoo. We are the only class that have Arts and Craft, and three other classes. We have multiplication, Divide, Adding. We have Morning Block. We play a game that nobody ever played before. It's bonus and jackpot prizes. We earn points by doing our work. And we play a lot games on Wednesdays we go out side to play games. We Read Reader Digest and Science Kramer. Just now Principal walked in. He is seeing how we work. He likes the class. The end

Under the "new words" condition one student wrote:

If I were President the U.S.A. there wouldn't be no Black Panthers and there wouldn't be no President in the city. And there would be no war. And policement wouldn't use clubs without trouble. And there wouldn't be no more school.

Under the "increasing the number of words used" condition a student wrote:

the Spring Thing Me and my Mother is going to the Spring Festival. My Mother is bringing a Cake to the Festival. We are going to sell horse and we sell dogs and sell fishes and we sell clowuns. We have fund makeing molds and we have fun makeing Wheelbarrels. I painted brick for the Festival. It is nice to make nice to bring a cake also. Eddie is bring a cake and some cookies for the Festival. We is selling necklaces braclert and rings. It is going to be a beautiful show at the Festival. We are selling our thing to put basketball hoops and baseball fields. We is going to eat food at the Festival. I am going to sell my Clown at the Festival. I would like to sell My clown for a one $1.00 piece.

The above stories are far from finished pieces of literature, but they do give the teacher and the child something to work from, and the material can be rewritten into a coherent and interesting story. Moreover, this procedure made the children enjoy writing.

PROGRAMMED LEARNING

Because of its ability to facilitate learning, programmed materials can save the teacher hours of work. Often, however, programmed materials are not easily available, owing to their cost, which can be considerable, or because of bureaucratic delay. Sometimes suitable materials are not available. In addition, many of the commercial materials tend to emphasize convergent thinking, that is, the one *correct* answer.

In some cases, teachers will have to make up their own materials, and it would be wise to review some of the principles and strengths of well-written programming.

Don Bushell from the University of Kansas Behavior Analysis Follow Through Program has stated that the use of a particular textbook series is likely to have a stronger influence on the shape and form of an instructional sequence than anything else. He defined an instructional sequence as a single lesson, a unit of several lessons, a text, or even an entire set of texts. He has worked out questions that can be used to judge if the materials lend themselves to good teaching.

a. Does the curriculum describe the terminal behavior?
b. Does the curriculum measure the students' entry levels?
c. Does the curriculum require frequent student responding?
d. Does the curriculum contain clear criteria for correct responses?
e. Does the curriculum contain check points and prescriptions?
f. Does the curriculum accommodate individual differences?

If the answers to these questions are affirmative, the materials will probably lead to greater learning on the part of pupils than curricula that do not require student responses, or that have unclear objectives, or do not describe the terminal objectives, and so forth.

If basal readers, for example, do not measure a student's entry level, the teacher will have to go through a lengthy series of trial-and-error procedures with each student in the class in order to be certain that each child is working at a level commensurate with his skill. When children are working with materials unsuitable for their level of development, they become bored, restless, and sometimes unruly.

Fortunately, most good programmed materials contain pre-tests so that appropriate placement is facilitated. Programmed materials also lend themselves to having students work at different levels, since even in a "homogeneously" grouped class there will be vast differences in skill areas between pupils. Aides and older children can also be more effective teachers when programmed materials are used.

In this day of the Xerox machine, teachers need not rely on commercially produced programs. Teachers can cut out sheets from old workbooks and make up their own material. A file of specific materials can be set up in this way. If Johnny has trouble with long and short vowels, it is extremely helpful if a set of work sheets is on hand. It is also quite helpful if answer sheets accompany the work sheets, because the child can correct his own work immediately.

It is most important for the teacher and the student to break the general skill or subject area into component parts. This can be done sometimes by means of end-of-chapter quizzes. A step-by-step analysis of exactly what the student has to know in order to solve a problem is helpful. In fact, the analysis itself will help to ensure learning.

If the teacher and students make an effort to add their own ideas to extend the curriculum materials, learning can be facilitated. A reading series, for example, can be improved by having each student pass a criterion test in order to enter a particular textbook series. The criterion can be as simple as that of reading a hundred-word passage in a reading text with less than five oral errors, and being able to answer four types of questions about the material read. These may be: a factual question, a question concerning a detail, a question concerning the main idea of a passage, and an inference-type question.

All of the above presupposes that the teacher knows the objectives of his or her lessons. This is crucial because (a) when goals are not specifically stated, teachers are not able to write specific lessons or arrange instructional materials in a way that will lead to specific knowledge, and (b) when goals are not specifically stated, the student will not know what is expected of him. In this last case he might give random answers, hoping to please the teacher rather than concentrating on the material to be learned. It is important to note in this context that reinforcement, no matter what form it takes, must be made contingent on the amount of work completed *correctly* or an approximation of the correct work.

If the reinforcement is placed only on the *amount* of work completed, a high percentage of errors will probably result. Also, if the criteria for demonstrating learning are not explicit, there will always be the danger that the student will *appear* to have learned the material.

As children progress through the grades, an important part of their curricula should be that they, too, learn how to set behavioral objectives. Children must be trained how to make meaningful choices and how to be held accountable for their learning. Neither teachers nor students should be allowed to absolve themselves of the responsibility of making decisions about objectives. Learning should result in a definite change, so that the student can do something he could not do before.

One book that describes in detail how to write behavioral objectives is that of Givner and Graubard.* It is recommended for both teachers and upper-grade students. It is important for teachers to give specific practice to children in this significant skill. It is equally important for that skill to be exemplified by the teacher's own practices.

A great deal of knowledge has been accumulated in the past five years about curriculum development. Some charismatic teachers have done a brilliant job of teaching without any technical background or programmed materials to help them—or, in some cases, hinder them. But for every great teacher there are probably twenty others who cannot accomplish this kind of teaching, or who lack teaching skills, and it is important to help these teachers and their pupils, too. Almost any teacher, in any classroom, can get more out of existing materials by building teaching objectives.

The more the children share in the setting of these objectives, the greater will be the likelihood of increasing learning. In addition, the greater will be the likelihood of reducing conflict within the classroom, as most children, like most adults, will work hard to pursue their own objectives. What is needed now is to match some of the exciting behavioral advances in curriculum development with programs and formats that explicitly use a behavioral approach.

The behavior-modification approach to education is perhaps best exemplified by a model sponsored by Dr.

* A. Givner and Paul Graubard, *A Handbook of Behavior Modification for the Classroom* (New York: Holt, Rinehart and Winston, 1974).

Don Bushell, Jr., and the University of Kansas. The aim of the program, called Behavior Analysis Follow Through, is quite explicit: to teach every child in the program basic academic skills. An additional aim is to develop autonomy within schools.

Bushell works with over 7,000 pupils in more than twelve different school districts stretching from the urban ghettos of New York City to Indian reservations in Montana and Arizona.

One criterion for initiating and maintaining the program is that the majority of the pupils come from families where the income is below the federally decreed poverty level. The second criterion is that everyone in the program—school districts, pupils, parents, and teachers—volunteer for participation. The rationale here is that when people are free to choose between alternatives they will undertake responsibility for their actions; thus free choice is superior to coercion when it comes to learning.

Accordingly, one of the primary tenets of the Behavior Analysis Follow Through Program is that learning without coercion and punishment is to be the rule. Invariably, this is greeted with cries of skepticism and dismay. The program is charged with naïveté and is accused of promoting license and anarchy. However, as Bushell has stated, the opposite of coercion is not anarchy or permissiveness. The alternative to coercion is the *right to choose*. Bushell speculates that perhaps choice is one of the prerequisites of peaceful and orderly change.

In order to establish school programs, Bushell suggests that key administrators should meet with their constituencies (parents and teachers) to *collaborate* in the establishment of goals. Once the objectives of an educational program are determined, then guidelines and procedures can be clarified. Teachers should be free to choose whether or not they want to work in such a program, and parents should have the right to choose whether or not they want their children to attend such a program.

He suggests that each grade level in the public schools should offer a variety of programs for the children in the school, with a clear explanation of the objectives and procedures to be followed. Planners of these programs should be responsible for announcing the criteria by which they want their program to be judged. Those programs which are the most effective, according to the criteria that parents approved, would attract more students.

Education should follow the example of a free marketplace, where advances in technology and product design are copied by competitive firms. The consumers of education would benefit if an advance in one educational program or system stimulated improvement in other programs. Educational practices could then be developed and refined to the satisfaction of parents and pupils, who now have little to say about the educational system.

In the Behavior Analysis Follow Through Program children are not forced to learn anything but can, of their own volition and at their own time, receive the needed reinforcement for individual learning. The fact that coercion is not used and that children are not under continual academic pressure is greeted with disbelief by most educators and parents, particularly since the achievement scores in this program are so impressive. It is through the teacher's openness and encouragement and the systematic engineering of the environment that the student engages in learning. Even the smallest increments of learning are acceptable and encouraged.

Another outstanding feature of the Behavior Analysis Follow Through Program is its ability to work with virtually *all* of the pupils enrolled. In one project in

New York City, which included more than seventeen classes over a period of six years, *not one child* was referred to a special-education class. Actuarial data would have predicted that almost twenty children would have been referred outside of the public school mainstream, and that the majority of the pupils would be deficient in basic skills. In the New York City program, the majority of the pupils who had been in the program since its inception were *above* grade level.

The primary reason for this extraordinary accomplishment probably lies in the fact that the curriculum was individualized so that each child could progress at his or her own pace. Therefore, no child had to be excluded from the mainstream because he or she "couldn't keep up with the class."

Another reason was the systematic reinforcement of positive behavior on the part of the child, and the ignoring of antisocial behavior.

For example, in one class a child, Leroy, was minutes late to class on the first day of school. He was in a third grade class. Leroy had already earned the reputation among teachers as a tough customer. Leroy got along well with peers but devastated teachers with wisecracks and insolence.

Leroy thought that he would get a reaction from the teacher by coming in late. When he arrived ten minutes after the late bell, his teacher said, "Your seat is over here, Leroy."

"How the hell you know my name, teach?"

Some of the members of the class tittered at Leroy's remark. Other classmates just sat in silent shock. His teacher, Mrs. Taylor, repeated, "Over here please, Leroy."

Leroy found a folder on top of his desk. "What's this stuff here, man?"

"That's some of your work for the day, Leroy."

"Work, you mean we gonna do work the first day of school? What kinda room you running here, man?"

There was no response from the teacher.

Leroy told the boy next to him in a loud stage whisper, "I ain't gonna do no work on the first day of school, man. Watch it blow the mind of old white eyes."

There was still no response from the teacher.

The other class members went to work. The teacher circulated among the students, praising them and giving them tokens for their work. She was giving them placement tests in order that they could be placed in material on their own level. Leroy slouched down in his seat in a posture that generally exasperated teachers. There was still no comment from Mrs. Taylor about his bad posture or the fact that he had not started to work yet. The rest of the class was now working quietly. Mrs. Taylor continued to reinforce the class for working so diligently.

"Hey man, what the hell you doing?" Leroy said to the youngster next to him.

"I'm finishing my work," was the reply.

"Big deal, man. You gonna be the teacher's pet you keep on working like that."

Many of the class members had finished the first page and had gone on to the second evaluation sheet. Leroy was bored and discouraged because he had not been able to get a rise out of the teacher. He opened his folder and looked at the first page. "Man, oh, man," he said. "This is a cinch. I can do that kinda stuff in a second." Leroy picked up his pencil and started to work on the page.

Mrs. Taylor bent over Leroy and said, "Very good. Here, let me give you another sheet. That page is too easy for you."

"You hear that, you cats? The lady say this work is

too easy for old Leroy. She gotta get him a harder page."

There was no reaction from the teacher or the class to Leroy's outburst. Mrs. Taylor returned with several new pages for Leroy. "Math must be your best subject, Leroy," she said.

Leroy took the new papers and started to work. He was now determined to show the teacher and the class how good he really was in math. He finished the work in ten minutes and raised his hand. The teacher was at his side and looked the papers over. "You got them all correct, Leroy. That work was still below your level. Let me get you something much harder. Your work is excellent. While I am finding some more work for you, could you please help Carlo for a minute? He is having trouble with some of his addition facts."

"Yeah, man, I can help him. I know those mothers cold, and Carlo, he's gonna learn 'em too." Leroy moved across the room and he and Carlo started practicing their number facts. Leroy would fire the questions at Carlo and Carlo would give Leroy the answer. Every time Carlo gave a correct answer Leroy would coax and encourage him. Toward the end of the period Leroy wrote down the facts that Carlo had missed the most and said, "You go home tonight and learn those, man. Tomorrow we gonna work on 'em some more." Leroy walked over to the teacher and said, "I think I gonna be able to teach 'em to him. I gotta drill him some more tomorrow."

Mrs. Taylor smiled and said, "Thank you, Leroy. I know you can really help Carlo."

When the bell rang, the students left the class for lunch. On the way out, Mrs. Taylor could hear Leroy say to one of his friends, "I think that class is gonna be okay."

In this program, if antisocial behavior persisted, such as shouting in crowded quarters, throwing things, hitting, and so forth, the teacher would "time out" the child.

"Time out" is a shorthand expression for "time out from positive reinforcement," which consists of ignoring the child and not giving him tokens for a specified period of time (usually from three to five minutes) immediately following the misbehavior. The other students are also reinforced for ignoring the antisocial child. The "time out" does not begin until the child is quiet and goes to another part of the room where he or she cannot interact with classmates or adults. After the "time out" elapses, the child is free again to enter the classroom activities, and to earn tokens if that kind of system is in operation.

When the children exchange their tokens for reinforcers, the child who has been timed out usually does not have enough tokens to purchase a desirable activity. Therefore he or she soon learns that there is a real advantage in appropriate behavior, while misbehavior results in simply being ignored.

Punishment is sometimes used, but only with the consent of the parent and an outside person who has to be convinced, by data compiled through systematic observations, that there is a compelling need for it to be employed. Punishment might consist of things like nonparticipation in a class trip, curtailment of TV privileges, isolation from the class, dining at a separate table, withholding of allowances (in collaboration with parents). Punishment is used very sparingly, however, and every effort is made to associate learning and school with positive consequences. All forms of abuse, be they ridicule, physical force, or simply delay, are prohibited in the classrooms. Teachers are taught to pay attention to the good things a child does.

By and large, studies have shown that when undesirable behavior on the part of the pupil gets teacher attention, this undesirable behavior will increase. In the same vein, when desirable behavior is reinforced, this type of behavior is increased. So the concern for reinforcing good behavior does not come out of a naïve, idealized child-development concept, but out of an empirical base.

The results of the Behavior Analysis Follow Through Program show that children from poverty backgrounds can be successful students and can achieve, on the average, at or above grade level in basic skills. The results are especially heartening when they are compared to the achievement scores of poor children from urban ghettos where reading levels, in particular, continue to decline.

The success of this program is also reflected in increased attendance rates and the fact that many families will not move from the district and the school in which their children are enrolled in this program. Traditional programs do not have the same holding power over the children.

When each aspect of the program is examined, the reason for its success becomes more apparent. All the participants in the educational process are involved in making the school experience a pleasurable and successful one.

When children enter the Behavior Analysis Follow Through Program in kindergarten, they are given tokens almost as soon as they hang up their coats or take their seats. The token, which can be a poker chip or a counting disc, at first has no meaning to the child. It is almost immediately exchanged for a piece of candy or a puzzle, or something else desirable. As the children engage in behavior conducive to learning—e.g., cooperating with their peers, following teacher instructions, looking at books—they are given additional tokens. These are also exchanged, almost immediately, for other books, snacks, the opportunity to play with animals, etc. Soon the children begin to realize that the tokens have value.

As the school year progresses, the children are divided into groups, and there is an adult or sometimes an older child working with each group. The children, during their "earn" or academic period, often use workbooks. When they have successfully completed their work, they are given more tokens. The tokens are always accompanied by praise.

At the end of an "earn" or academic period, the tokens are exchanged for things of value to the children. They may be activities such as playing with hamsters, receiving additional reading or mathematics instruction, writing on the board, learning script, watching television, playing jump rope.

At the end of the exchange period, which consumes the tokens the child has earned, another "earn" period is scheduled, and the child has an opportunity to receive more tokens by learning and displaying new skills.

The classes are grouped according to age because of the nature of public schools, but there are no assumptions made about the relationship between age and ability. Each child is given curriculum material based upon placement tests, and he or she is then encouraged to work as rapidly as his or her abilities and interests permit.

The individually paced programmed materials allow the children to record their responses in a way that permits them and their teacher to see what is being accomplished. Students have the opportunity to make many responses, and the teachers can then see where the problems lie and begin to work with these responses.

When programmed materials are not used, individualized instruction is still employed, by converting traditional materials into a new format that allows the children to work at their own rate toward specific objectives. For example, group reading texts can be used individually. Non-textbooks can also be used; the necessity here is that a clear-cut criterion for mastery of a definite objective is outlined.

Motivation is also maximized in the Behavior Analysis Follow Through Program by allowing each child to choose his or her own reinforcer, which is given for performance. A minimum of six activities follow each "earn" period, and teachers are constantly encouraged to add new items of appropriate interest.

Another important principle of the program is that the shaping of behavior is effective only when it is maintained by more natural kinds of reinforcers than tokens. Reading becomes a reinforcer when skills have become solidified and children want to read on their own. The children should be able to *choose* reading as one of their reinforcing activities. When that happens, it can be safely assumed that the program has been effective.

Teachers need to be given instruction in this type of teaching and in how to use the curriculum materials. Instructional staff are taught to "catch" the children being good and to reward appropriate behavior with tokens and praise. In order to develop this kind of teaching ability, it has been found necessary to have in-service training courses.

In Bushell's behavior-modification program, every ten classrooms are provided with a full-time teacher-trainer whose sole job is to go to all of the classrooms and make detailed observations of the interactions between teachers and pupils, or between pupils themselves. Working from a data observation sheet, which helps to document whether teachers are reinforcing appropriate behavior and whether instruction leads to new behavior on the part of pupils, the trainer gives feedback to the teachers on the specifics of the classroom interactions.

The trainer and the teacher then collaborate in thinking up possibly effective teaching procedures, and these concrete ideas are put into practice. Data is taken on the implementation and effectiveness of these procedures. Empirical observation, which outside observers can give, is crucial to the development of the teacher at this stage.

The trainer's role is one that could be played by teachers or administrative staff, if they were trained for it. Training could consist of completion of a behavior-modification program. Certainly the trainer should be able to demonstrate that he or she can modify, in a positive way, the behavior of those in need of help. Most university-based behavior-modification programs already require students to write up their experiences in this way. The trainer should be thoroughly knowledgeable in curriculum development, remedial methods, pedagogy, and methods of observing behavior. The trainer should also be able to help teachers implement activities that will lead to increased learning for the children.

One key aspect to the training program is the use of demonstration classrooms. Rather than rely on university training only, which almost everyone agrees is inadequate, certain classrooms, which meet specific criteria, are selected as in-service training classrooms.

When untrained teachers come into the program, or if any teachers are having difficulty with certain procedures, they can go to the demonstration classroom and observe the procedures in question. They practice the skills in the demonstration classroom and receive corrective feedback from the demonstration teacher and trainer. When the skills have been perfected in the demonstration classroom, teachers have the opportunity to employ them immediately in their own classrooms. This is done with the assistance of the trainer.

For example, Nancy R. was in her second year of teaching first grade. Her first year of teaching was in a regular school program, where she was rated as an average teacher. In the Follow Through first grade Nancy did a fine job with those students who learned quickly and displayed appropriate school manners. She did not do as well with children who had difficulty learning, and she had an especially hard time with some of the aggressive boys in her class. She took obstreperous and defiant behavior as a personal affront and would get into power struggles with some of the children. For example, she would ask the children to put away the blocks after a building period. If a child dawdled or would not put the blocks away, Nancy would begin to holler at the child, and threaten to tell his mother. Usually the child reacted by cursing at the teacher and further defiance. Nancy would get even angrier and would sometimes shake the child to get the desired results. While this technique would sometimes work, it would often leave her breathless and so angry that she could not devote her full attention to teaching the class after the incident was over.

The trainer measured how many times such incidents occurred and how long it took to get the blocks back in place. The trainer then suggested that Nancy observe how cleaning-up periods were handled in the demonstration class. In this class contingencies were placed on prompt and neat putting-away of material. If all the blocks were neatly stacked away by the time the bell on the timer rang (it was set for five minutes), the class would have the chance to view a filmstrip. Nancy practiced this technique in the demonstration class and then used it in her own class. Within three days the rate of nagging went from nine times a session to zero times a session, and the time taken to put away the blocks decreased from twelve minutes to five minutes. Eventually the children were able to put the blocks away within three minutes.

Most teacher-training programs are given in universities and consist of fifteen-week courses, in which the learner seldom gets the opportunity to practice skills under supervision. Skills that have just been learned should be practiced immediately. Also, not surprisingly, the children fare much better under the system of demonstration classrooms than when their teachers wait for summer courses to pick up new skills.

Another important aspect of the program is the feedback, which comes in part from the trainer who observes and documents the classroom interactions. Problems that arise in the classroom can be handled immediately by the trainer. Data sheets help to specify exactly where children are having difficulty with the curriculum. This information, the meticulous records on pupil progress, and the amount of time spent in instruction are all extremely helpful in making each teacher's development concrete.

Many teachers use the classroom as a podium for telling pupils about their own personal lives, or for marching them from classroom to bathroom and back again. The amount of instructional time in classrooms therefore varies enormously. Weekly reports on specific time application prove invaluable. If teachers and administrators wait for year-end tests (and these achievement tests are not given in many primary grades) in order to get information on pupil progress, it will be too late to help students who had difficulty. The use of continuous data enables appropriate changes to come about when they are most needed.

Bushell has stated that in one district the average kindergarten child in several project classrooms received only a little over two hours of reading instruction per week. When the progress records were shown to the teachers and student needs detailed, reading instruction nearly doubled.

Most teachers in the program now keep their records posted in the classroom, so that what transpires is open to all concerned. This kind of openness is also extremely important. In the name of professionalism, records are often kept from the people who are most directly concerned, namely, teachers, children, and parents. If information is withheld from these people, they can do very little to change a situation, since they lack appropriate data.

In addition to the amount of time spent on instruction, careful records are kept on pupil progress. Teachers record the number of the page and the name of the book on which the child is working at the end of every week. Each group of books in the curriculum series has accompanying charts.

On the vertical axis of the chart, the page of the book, broken into approximately equal intervals, is listed. Each week the number of children who have progressed to each step is listed. This gives the teacher, pupils, administrators, and parents a concise look at class progress. Since the teacher already has ongoing lists of where each child is in each curriculum area, information on individuals can be provided as well. Any breakdown in progress can be immediately noted, and the trainer has something specific with which to work, together with the teacher. Faults can lie with curriculum materials, methods of instruction, the kinds of reinforcement used, or any one of a number of factors. However, a clear look can be taken at each one of these factors while there is still time to do something about them.

This system of graphing has been somewhat superseded by computer progress records compiled by the University of Kansas. This system provides targets for the children, calculates the ratio of successful instructional sequences, and so on. This, of course, is too expensive for any one classroom to use. The chart above, on the other hand, can be adapted by any teacher who takes the time to organize instructional objectives.

BEHAVIOR ANALYSIS 197 – 197

School: Teacher: Subject: Arithmetic
          Assistant Teacher: Grade: Curriculum: Sets And Numbers

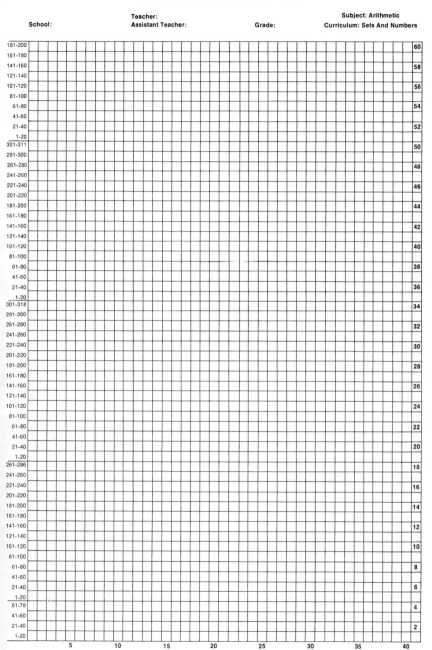

PROJECT:

WEEKS:

A final major aspect of the Kansas program is the *type* of curriculum used and accordingly the teaching procedures that are employed. Instructional objectives may be as varied as learning how to stand in line at the water fountain, or learning how to pronounce polysyllabic words. With either of these goals, criteria are set up so that the teacher and the pupil will know when they have accomplished these goals. Curriculum is employed, whether it is teacher-constructed or commercially purchased, which states what the child can do as a result of his teacher's efforts. The curriculum must also require frequent responses on the part of the child and contain clear-cut criteria as to correctness to which both the pupil and the teacher can respond. The materials must also provide for periodic testing of gains in achievement.

There are often distinct disadvantages to programmed materials, and these must be considered. In the Sullivan programmed material (an individualized reading series published by McGraw-Hill), for example, the answers are given on the left-hand side of the page. The pupil is expected to cover up these answers while he or she completes the problem, and then use the answers only to correct the work that is finished. Sometimes, even inadvertently, pupils copy the answers. To counteract this, teachers are instructed to give tokens only for work done orally. With this emphasis on oral responses the teacher can quickly ascertain the child's knowledge, and there is also no incentive for "cheating," since the reward is only for the oral answer, and not for the written one. Teachers use a "red line" procedure in this part of the program, which consists of underlining every fifth or tenth frame with a red pencil. When a child comes to the underlined problem, he or she will treat it as a red light and stop. At this point the pupil contacts the teacher, who reviews the previous frames and makes sure the child can generalize his answers from the programmed material.

In this way, the teacher can make sure that the child really understands the solution to a problem. It is the teacher's responsibility to make the material interesting enough and reinforcement appealing enough so that the child will decide it is worthwhile to work. And there are definite targets and skills toward which the child and the teacher can work. Product as well as process is stressed.

The complexity and individualization inherent in this program make it virtually impossible for only one teacher to function effectively in a classroom with approximately thirty children. Thus parents and aides are used as teachers in the classroom.

At the outset, the program is explained to the parents, and they are free to enroll their children in Follow Through or in other school programs. The parents then form an advisory committee and participate fully in all discussions about the program. They are invited to state their views about personnel in the program and make recommendations for the hiring and firing of teachers. While legally this prerogative belongs to the principal, the recommendations of the parents are considered.

The University of Kansas Behavior Analysis model also has a training component attached to the parent program. Parents are trained to work as teachers in the classroom. One aspect of the training is to help people focus on child achievement. Parents are taught that the effectiveness of the entire staff—be they teacher, administrator, aide, or parent—is based on student progress. By training staff to focus on achievement data, criteria that are not relevant to the student's cognitive growth, such as the teacher's race or religion, or dress codes, cannot be confused with the real issue of performance.

Children work best in personalized situations, but even in small groups, instruction must be centered on the individual. Heterogeneous groupings are the rule; there is no delusion that children with even the same reading scores on a standardized test need to learn the same kinds of skills. Follow Through accepts the fact that each child is unique, and therefore any attempt at homogeneous grouping is impossible.

It is imperative, then, that parents and aides are given instruction in teaching methods. This is accomplished directly, by having them teach, under the supervision of the trained teacher, real children, and with real academic material. Their work is scrutinized and there is not more than a two- or three-minute delay between their performance and the response to their performance. Teaching behavior is noted with great accuracy—for example: number of contacts with children, number of questions that prompted further behavior on the part of the pupils, number of positive reinforcements, number of reinforcements of antisocial behavior, etc.

Parents and aides also observe the demonstration classrooms with the teacher-trainer and trainees take the same counts on the teaching staff that were taken on themselves. In addition, the trainees meet with the demonstration-room staff to share in the planning of lessons.

Thus learning is individualized for adults as well as for children. The double standard of teacher-training, where professors and administrators talk about individualization but treat teachers as a listening, nonparticipative audience, is eliminated. People learn from what their teachers *do,* and not from what they *say* should be done. It is the behavior of the individual that counts, not verbal statements about behavior. The data from this program show that the basic goals that were set by the administrators, parents, and teachers have been reached. When the goals are attained, the participants in the program meet to set new goals, and again the behavioral methods employed in the program can be quite helpful in attaining their new goals.

4

Teaching Adaptive Behavior

The technology of behavior modification can also be used to promote the goals of the free schools. Alternative schools were founded because of the pressing need to develop programs that children would enjoy, through which they would learn important skills, and within which they would learn to develop autonomy.

The difficulty encountered in discussions with many free-school proponents is that the idea of autonomy is discussed without either empirical or theoretical support. As Dr. Thomas Brigham, a research psychologist from Washington State University, has noted, free-schoolers assume that "autonomy is good; it is innate; and it will flower if merely encouraged."

Some of the favorite terms that free-school proponents use are "automony," "spontaneity," "freedom of action," and "inner-directed behavior." But the mere abstraction of the words *autonomy* and *spontaneity* do not help us distinguish between the activity of the creative artist and the psychotic.

Autonomous behavior is a more functional term when the subject, the setting, and the audience are each defined. This is why Brigham has suggested that, instead of discussing autonomy abstractly, we should consider actual autonomous situations.

An autonomous setting in the school is a situation where a pupil has the opportunity to choose between alternative activities without coercion. One way of achieving more autonomy for students and teachers is through behavior-modification systems.

Dr. Charles Salzberg and Dr. Sarah Rule of the University of Kansas and the Colorado Springs Community School have applied behavior-modification procedures within a free school.

In 1969 a group of parents from Colorado Springs, Colorado, opened their school as an alternative to the local public school system. They rejected the idea of their children sitting in neat rows while passively listening to the teacher and being forced to while away hours and days without being able to talk, chew gum, or disagree with the teacher.

These parents wanted their children's learning to be pleasant as well as productive. They wanted their children to feel the exuberance that scholarship and curiosity can bring. They wanted them to learn to interact with other children as well as with their teachers. And they wanted them to leave school with the realization that learning is fun, and that it is not bounded by the walls of the classroom.

From its inception, the Colorado Springs Community School was modeled after the free schools. The age range of the pupils was from five to fourteen and all classes were voluntary. Teachers were there to facilitate things for the children and to provide guidance, as well as to provide explanations of subject matter and materials. Frequent camping and field trips were planned and open expression of thoughts and feelings was encouraged.

Despite the best intentions of parents and teachers, Salzberg and Rule found that academic work was becoming an infrequent activity. Also, despite a favorable teacher-pupil ratio and sincere and competent young men and women as teachers, the children were not acquiring skills.

Salzberg and Rule also found an increase in rude social behavior. Little respect was shown for the privacy and property of others. Older children would terrorize younger children and cliques were formed that were abusive toward nonmembers.

Group meetings were held to discuss these problems, and the group agreed that such behavior should not be permitted in the school. But the verbal statements led to no change in behavior. The school, in spite of its professed aim to give children greater freedom, was becoming a place where individuals had even fewer rights than in traditional schools. The children were becoming fearful for their safety. What had been started with *Summerhill* as an inspiration became, in reality, *Lord of the Flies*.

The problems encountered in the Colorado Springs Community School are probably not unique and could account for the high mortality rate of free schools. Pupil and staff turnover in free schools is great, and most children and teachers probably find it easier simply to leave than to fight for a solution.

The situation is aggravated by what Jonathan Kozol calls the intellectual and moral neuterism of many of the teachers. Because of their dislike for structure and direction, many teachers (and students) have taken the easiest way out and have tried allowing structure to evolve by itself. But structure and freedom are intertwined, and freedom sought in this way is often very different from what was originally hoped for.

School participants who sought complete freedom of access to materials and activities and a similar freedom in their application did not anticipate that temporarily quitting a certain project could mean finding it destroyed when they returned. They did not realize that freedom of movement can also imply the ability to disturb others, or that freedom of expression can mean intimidation.

The Colorado school found that trips into the community, guest speakers, etc., were possible only if teachers and students acted responsibly. Volunteers who were abused or treated rudely seldom returned. Places that had welcomed the school turned down requests for permission to visit again, and the destruction of property and materials led to a depletion of resources that became acute. As a result, severe restrictions had to be placed on materials.

The gradual disintegration of the school, and the erosion of personal freedom that accompanied it, led the parents and staff to try a different tack. Instead of complete freedom and the assumption that responsibility would ensue, *specific* freedoms were given to individual children *only* after each child had demonstrated responsible behavior.

The wisdom of this approach was tested through mathematics instruction. It was felt that mathematics was an area in which the children needed systematic instruction, as their achievement in this area was low in relation to their chronological ages. The children were therefore given free time when they maintained satisfactory rates of progress in their mathematics period.

Salzberg and Rule used the Suppes series *Sets and*

Numbers as the basic curriculum for this area and transcribed the material onto ditto sheets. Each sheet contained no more than two concepts, which were defined as a new type of problem or a new format for a problem. A quiz was given for every ten concepts, and children were required to achieve an 80 percent accuracy level on each quiz before they could move on to new material. Instruction was individualized, and each child had to have his or her work corrected and pass the proficiency level of 80 percent before being allowed to leave the classroom.

Although this teaching method was finally decided upon, a number of others were tried. One method was to have students complete a minimum of one page, after which they were allowed to leave. A variation required the students to record their progress on a feedback sheet. Another included completing the one-page-a-day requirement, plus passing a quiz. If the children did not pass the quiz, they had to stay in the math class during the entire week for the length of the math period. The students continued to chart their own progress during this procedure. A further method required students to take two quizzes per week, but if they passed the first quiz on Tuesday and the second quiz during the last half of the week, they did not have to attend class at all for the remainder of the week. An additional restriction on this group was that they were not allowed to disturb the students who were attending class. Finally, for a very short period, students had to come to class, but they were not required to do any work and they could leave whenever they wanted to. In addition to the objective evidence accumulated, questionnaires were given to the students asking them to indicate which method of teaching they preferred.

A comparison of the results of the teaching conditions was clear-cut, and from the viewpoint of both parents and teachers the results were also encouraging. During the one-page-a-day minimum requirement, the children progressed at the rate of one grade level per academic year. During the one-quiz-a-week teaching method, the children progressed at a rate that would have allowed them to cover two years of mathematics during the academic year. In the two-quizzes-per-week procedure, this rate jumped to three and a half times to four times as high as the normal rate of one year's progress for every academic year.

Salzberg and Rule also reported that there were many more instances of cooperation and voluntary home-work completion, and an entirely different atmosphere in the school. This procedure was helpful with nineteen out of the twenty students enrolled in the program. It was felt that free time did not serve as a reinforcer for one child who had a long history of negative relationships with other children in the group. The students said that they liked the heavy work loads because they were matched with increasing opportunities for free time.

As a result of the new system, students began to arrive in class early—something they had never done before. They brought pencils to class, asked for help, and worked on homework and studied, even when it was not required.

The project was summarized by Salzberg and Rule as follows:

> *Those who are interested in conducting free schools will come, in time, to recognize, as we did, that there is more to the creation of a free environment than removing adult supervision. Freedom can exist in a school only to the extent that the students in that school can produce and maintain that responsible behavior, but only when access to those freedoms is made contingent upon that responsible behavior.*

BEHAVIORAL APPROACHES TO CURRICULUM

The behavioral approach to curriculum has been extended into a whole system of instruction by Dr. Alan Cohen, formerly of Yeshiva University in New York City. The key to instruction, Cohen believes, can be found in the interaction between teacher style, pupil style, and the resources found in the classroom. As teacher behavior varies, there will be changes in pupil behavior and resources. In a systems approach, these three components are controlled, with a resulting control over instructional outcomes.

Cohen's system is now being used in scores of school districts throughout the country. The research results are impressive in that thousands of pupils, many of them greatly disadvantaged, have achieved a high degree of academic success. Cohen's program makes it possible for a regular classroom teacher to deal effectively with a wide range of student abilities.

The system, designed for use in grades one through fourteen, is usually housed in a reading center, which can accommodate whole classes, and where pupils work on *prescribed reading activities* designed to teach *specific skills*. The heart of the system lies in the more than five hundred instructional objectives (I.O.'s) that Cohen and his colleagues have culled from the vast amount of published material on reading.

Each I.O. is matched to a specific reading material, which facilitates the acquisition of the skills in question. The skills range from the most basic (after hearing two or more words, the student indicates whether the words are the same or different) to highly complex ones. For example: after reading a selection, the student identifies statements from the selection as being fact (true) or opinion (not necessarily true); or, given a set of alternatives, the student indicates if the alternatives represent a real choice (all possible choices) or a false choice (some choices omitted).

When a pupil arrives at the reading center, he is given an Instructional Objectives Test, which aids the teacher in determining his strengths and weaknesses. The tests, in turn, are keyed to a catalog of objectives, which contains the exact materials (from a wide variety of sources) that will help the pupil master the objectives. A method of teaching the skill is also prescribed for the student. If the student does not master the objective, new materials and different methods are prescribed. After demonstrating mastery of the prescribed objectives, the pupil is given new I.O. tests. Based upon these findings, he will receive a new prescription, which again is specific to his present needs. This process can aid a student at any point in his learning career, and it remains continuous throughout the year. An explicit reinforcement system can be tied to mastery of the instructional objectives, but a reinforcement system does not have to be used. Most of the materials are self-correcting and lend themselves easily to graphing and record-keeping.

Such a system may conjure up for some an image of regimented children and a straitjacketed instructor. Nothing can be further from the truth. The reading centers can be made attractive and appealing. They contain hundreds and hundreds of books and activities from over sixty different publishers' materials. Students quite often use non-textbooks, which are chosen especially to appeal to their age group and performance level. Since the books contain stories and information on hundreds of topics, it is an extremely rare student who cannot find *some* material to interest him.

While the teacher's activities are somewhat prescribed by the system, the teacher is still able to select materials to cover a wide range of skills, and to use different methods to teach these skills. The teacher acts more as a diagnostician and instructional manager than as a talker or lecturer. He or she shares in each student's aesthetic enjoyment and learning skills, and the student can grow without the teacher being the sole dispenser of knowledge.

One of the reading centers we visited looked like the arrangement on page 89.

There was no rigid seating pattern, and children worked wherever they were comfortable. Two charts with instructions were posted. The first was labeled "Getting Started" and contained these instructions: (1) Get your folder. (2) Check your prescription. (3) Select your material. (4) Write your name and complete the answers. (5) Check your answers. (6) Correct your answers. (7) Fill in your progress plotter.

The second chart was placed in front of the tape decks and said: "Take a tape; take an answer sheet; take a scoring card after you have finished your work; mark your own work."

These charts were helpful in the establishment of routines in the class that allowed children to work independently and sometimes in groups. Much of the material was self-grading, and there were a good many checks built into the material allowing the teacher to test the child's mastery of the material. The amount of clerical work that occupied the teacher was minimal compared to the time spent on instruction.

This system has the added advantage of building in teacher and school accountability. Skills are well defined and the instruction is sequential. After an intensive assessment, which is available from Cohen at Educational Systems Division, Random House in New York City, it was concluded:

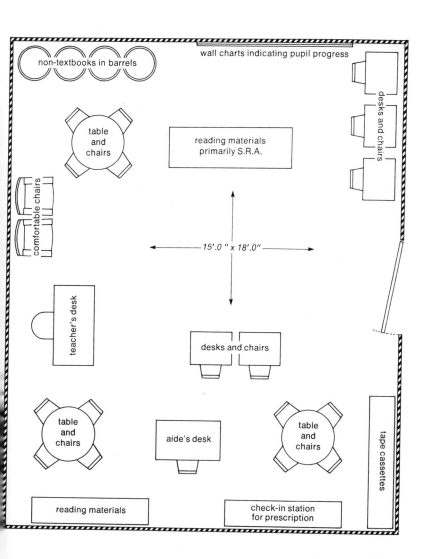

non-textbooks in barrels

wall charts indicating pupil progress

desks and chairs

table
and
chairs

reading materials
primarily S.R.A.

comfortable chairs

15'.0 " x 18'.0"

teacher's desk

desks and chairs

table
and
chairs

aide's desk

table
and
chairs

tape cassettes

reading materials

check-in station
for prescription

1. Good intensive reading instruction leads to high achievement gains, regardless of the socioeconomic background of the learner.
2. The systematic application of learning principles must be an integral part of a teaching program.
3. Curriculum reform is considerably more than merely changing from one set of curriculum materials to another. Curriculum redesign calls for a redeployment of instructional resources, physical topography, manpower, and money.
4. Instructional systems can be purchased and implemented at a lower cost than "programs" that merely consist of buying publisher's materials.
5. Teachers can be trained, at no great cost to the school budget, to use a systems approach, and they can be accountable for instruction.
6. Instructional systems do not call for more work on the part of the teacher. Many of the materials are self-pacing and self-instructing. They do call for a different role for the teacher.

CURRICULUM AND ADAPTATION

Our present society is employing fewer members in production roles and more members in service roles, where the ability to adapt to new people and new conditions is paramount. What is needed today is a curriculum to teach adaptive skills. As the pace of our social structure changes, we will need more flexible members of society, not those who cannot think for themselves or who can be coerced and cowed.

One method for increasing adaptive behavior has been devised by Dr. Salvador Minuchin, a social psychiatrist at the Philadelphia Child Guidance Clinic. Minuchin has stated that many lower-socioeconomic-status children are socialized so that they are unable to meet the school's implicit expectations of social and cognitive conduct, and the coercive methods used to socialize these children lead to an inhibition of behavior that is often followed by explosive outbursts rather than an ability to adapt.

Where parental control is unpredictable, the child is handicapped in learning the rules of socialization. The child finds it difficult to determine what parts of his or her behavior are inappropriate and learns to search out the limits of permissible behavior by observing the parent's mood.

Among many lower-socioeconomic-status children, much of the parent-child interaction is ineffective, and this increases the burden of an overtaxed mother. As a result, limits become even more erratic. Minuchin states that children respond to the erratic messages of their parents by behaving in ways that will reorganize their own "known" environment. The child controls the contact of his mother by behaving in a way that is sure to bring a decisive and swift response from her, usually a negative one involving physical force. The child spends a great deal of time searching out the reaction of others, but is unable to recognize the manipulative aspect of his or her own reaction to a given situation and the importance of his or her own behavior in an interaction. In many of the families Minuchin studied, the children were often ignored because of the sheer size of the family, and they implicitly learned that words by themselves will not be heard, and the intensity of an action or sound is more persuasive than the logic of an argument.

Conflict is often resolved by the escalation of threats and counter-threats between adult and child. The specific *content* of a discussion is of such secondary importance that a state of irresolution is almost unavoidable. Family members do not expect to be heard and can only assert themselves by yelling. They have not been trained to formulate questions so that additional information can be gathered, nor are the subtleties and complexities of questions appreciated. Themes are not developed to their logical conclusion, and the child is trained to pay more attention to the person with whom he is interacting than to the content or structure of the theme he is discussing.

This style of interaction violates the implicitly held demands of the school, where order and discipline are the tools used to scrutinize content. The child, attempting to cope with the anxiety caused by the school, responds to the teacher as if he were a threatening parent.

Minuchin and his co-workers feel that much of the disruptive behavior in classrooms can be interpreted as an attempt to repair relations with an authority figure, and to re-create the known environment under which the child operates at home. This is interpreted by the teacher, however, as aggressive behavior, which often results in the child's being punished and/or removed from the school.

To counteract this type of socialization, an intervention curriculum was designed by Minuchin and two educators, Pamela Chamberlain and Paul Graubard, in order to help children learn how to learn in school. The goal of the project was to teach children how to survive in school and master some of the interpersonal relations and cognitive themes that schools demand.

It was explained to the children who were in a special project that they would be taught a curriculum that would help them to do well in school, even if their teacher did not like them. (Prior to this, the children had believed that doing well in school could only be accomplished if the teacher liked them. They felt that a good grade represented how well a teacher liked a particular student.) A procedure was used in which the students assumed the alternate roles of both participant and observer. Observers were placed behind a one-way mirror, and the children were trained to rate the other children's behavior as learners. These observers were specifically taught to enumerate the behavior that either enhanced or interfered with learning.

The focus of this project was to train children to judge learning behavior rather than conforming behavior. Points were awarded to the learners by the judges, and specific reasons had to be given for points lost or won. A small amount of money was awarded for each point earned, and the judges received points (and thereby money) when their records, derived independently, coincided with that of the teacher's record.

The curriculum consisted of communication skills intended to unravel the process of the classroom for the children. Lessons were sequentially planned and included listening, staying on a topic, taking turns, telling simple stories, asking meaningful questions, categorizing and classifying information, and appreciating the roles of others. This last aspect enabled them to learn what behavior to expect from others.

Games were the medium through which many of these skills were taught, and the bulk of these games was selected from primary-grade activities, even though the children were considerably older. The games themselves incorporated elements of the children's lives and were thus easier for them to relate to than abstractions.

In this project, the children were first taught listening skills. They started with Simon Says, a game with which they were already familiar. The process of the game was explained, and it was pointed out that the game is won by listening and learning how to pay attention to *what* was said, rather than to *how* it was said.

The children also had the opportunity to listen to messages on the telephone and were required to repeat these messages exactly as they had been heard. The children were quite adept at reading expressions and at getting the gist of a message, but they found it much harder to remember without face-to-face contact. The differences between guessing and careful listening were then discussed, and this became obvious to all the students.

Series of numbers were read aloud to the children, and they were asked to tell what the second number was or which number was highest or lowest. A discussion followed about what it felt like while waiting to speak, or having to keep directions in mind. These, of course, are common demands in classroom learning.

Noise was introduced to the lessons *as a result* of the usual style of living "known" by the boys. The children participated in a game in which one child would tell a story and the rest of the children would make noise. Some children helplessly repeated phrases in hoping to be heard, and others tried to outshout their classmates. The result was usually chaos, and the implications of such noise for classroom learning were made obvious. The students were not admonished for loud disturbances, but they did lose points for the incorrect answers that usually accompanied noise-making.

An additional part of the curriculum consisted in taking turns. To teach this skill, familiar nursery rhymes were divided up, with each child assigned a part. The difficulties of listening for one's own cue, taking turns in speaking, and waiting for the other person to speak were highlighted and practiced, with rewards accompanying successful performance. It was felt that the familiarity of the material was reassuring to the children and helped them to think that they could succeed in their tasks.

Later sessions included unfamiliar stories made up by the teacher, which the children were to repeat in parts.

Each had to listen for a cue, decide when he could begin, and tell everyone when he was finished. Discussion was initiated about the logical sequence of stories and conversations, and the children were able to cue one another in later sessions when they found someone rambling away from the topic under discussion.

After a few sessions, the mechanics of the process were incorporated into the children's behavior. The children were judged and were starting to judge each other in positive terms, which was a relatively unfamiliar experience to them. The monetary rewards and the adult and peer approval motivated the children to master the curriculum.

Conceptual skills were also taught through the medium of games. I Spy and Twenty Questions were very helpful, since they emphasize categorizing. At the beginning, the answers given by the children were too concrete. For example, one question was "I am thinking about a person who works in the school. Who is that person?" A typical answer was, "Mrs. Jones." Different people were named until the students used up all twenty questions. It was eventually discovered by the class that a simple question like "Is the person a female?" or "Does she work on the second floor?" would significantly reduce the number of questions needed and result in winning the game. They began to consider which questions would help them and which were irrelevant.

After the children became more adept at ordering their own universe and started to "win" by giving the correct answers, they were taught to "win" in interactions with adults. These skills were taught through the medium of role-playing.

They were expected to "win" in these interactions by paying attention to the content as well as to the form of the messages, by asking direct and relevant questions instead of exploding in rage, by waiting for their turn to speak, by signaling the other person when he might begin, and so on.

The children took the roles they usually played with teachers and other persons in authority, and then they each in turn took the role of one of those authority figures. Minuchin and his colleagues describe one child who played the role of a guidance counselor and said to another child, "I'm willing to listen to you, but I expect you to let me finish."

Although the evidence consisted of clinical judgment rather than detailed observations and counts of behavior, the authors of this study concluded that role-playing made the skills the children learned applicable to their own lives. The students were more cognizant of their own actions and could label them with a fair degree of accuracy. In the final role-playing sessions, the children were not only quick to label mistakes that their peers had made but, more importantly, they were able to help each other correct their mistakes and try new approaches in situations that were unsuccessful.

An important aspect of the project was the judging that took place. The students were trained to differentiate between nuances of behavior, whereas before they could only judge the extremes. Because they were conscious of being observed and received a positive reward for their appropriate behavior, the children became more objective about their own behavior. Often they would stop themselves in the middle of a fight, realizing that they would not be able to listen attentively if they were fighting. An apology would be made to the "judges" behind the one-way mirror, and the combatants would slow down their activities so that the judges could see their behavior more clearly.

Part of the success of this project was also based on

the fact that the teacher and the pupils were working together for the same goals. The students, who were in a special-education track, wanted to move into the mainstream of education and also wanted to learn how to learn.

The teacher was careful to use familiar material with the students and introduced new themes only when old ones had been learned and practiced. The teacher constantly shifted from abstract to concrete demands and also de-emphasized the role of power figure. Rewards were given only for performance; the teacher subtly pointed out that the "judges" were their peers, and that they themselves would be "judges." The teacher related to the students not as a friend or authority figure but as a highly differentiated adult who was skilled in guiding children through tasks. After the mechanics of the task were learned, the teacher emphasized the relationship between personal behavior and interpersonal results.

This specific emphasis should play a major part in curriculum construction if schools are to succeed in teaching adaptation skills to their pupils. The program described in the California ecological-behavioral projects (see chapter 2) worked explicitly with this theme. Children can be taught to set behavioral goals for themselves that can be pinpointed and measured.

Once the child has learned *how* to set objectives, it is a relatively simple matter for him to count his own behavior and to see the effect of his behavior on the behavior of others. Direct cause-and-effect relationships can be effectively established in the area of interpersonal relationships.

Much of the behavior-modification literature reported in the *Journal of Applied Behavior Analysis* details procedures that may be used to teach this kind of curriculum to children. It is, of course, best if teachers and children have mutual or at least complementary goals. A great deal of research has shown that pupils learn more if they have a choice in selecting both the subject matter and the type of reinforcement they receive; the teacher and child should make these "negotiations" as early as possible in their school careers.

Many children who fight authority in the classrooms and in the streets do so because their repertoire of skills in working with other people is underdeveloped. They are both unable to foresee the consequences of their own behavior and helpless to know how to make changes when necessary. This is particularly true of adolescent delinquents who have been placed in specific roles by their peers and teachers.

Dr. Martha Lewis and some of her colleagues at the University of Kansas have adapted a SOCS model, first developed by Dr. Jan Roosa, a clinical psychologist in private practice in Kansas City. SOCS is an abbreviated form of the following components: S, identifying a specific conflict *situation;* O, determining the possible *options* that the youngster has; C, identifying the probable *consequences* of his own behavior; and S, *simulating* the desired behavior that will help him gain the options he wishes to achieve.

Using this basic model, Lewis and her colleagues taught adaptive skills to a group of youngsters who were on probation. The youngsters were taught in a class situation, and mastery of the skills was one of the conditions the youngsters had to meet to get off probation.

The students were trained in communication skills, which consisted of:

1. Helping the student to state his own position or desires.
2. Requesting feedback from the other person involved in the transaction.

3. Recognizing and stating the difference between the two positions.
4. Suggesting solutions of the problems by stating which options were more desirable.

In short, the pupils were taught how to negotiate.

Their training package consisted of the definition and explanation of specific behaviors on the part of the trainers, and then one trainer acted as a model of the specific behaviors. Next, the students simulated conflict situations, and this was followed by reinforcement of appropriate student behavior. Specific suggestions for improving performance were also given at this time. Videotapes were used so that the students might see how well they accomplished their tasks. The cycle was repeated by a rotating group of students. Finally, the students practiced their skills in a simulated real-life situation with a complete stranger.

An example of their approach can be seen in the following situation, taken from one of their reports. Situation: You want to go somewhere, but your parents will not let you go. The options are then identified. They may be: (1) Tell them to go to hell; (2) go anyway; (3) ask them why they object or refuse; (4) ask them to take you and pick you up; (5) express disappointment and try for another time; (6) make them feel guilty; (7) sneak out. The consequences might be: (1) getting slapped across the room; (2) earning the privilege of going out; (3) getting grounded; (4) getting a reasonable explanation; (5) parents changing mind; (6) staying home and feeling depressed; (7) parents calling police.

Once the desired consequence is determined by the student, the matching option is simulated by peers, with one child playing the role of the learner and another playing the role of an authority figure.

Lewis and her co-workers found that the students were able to apply the skills they had learned to strangers, new teachers, and other adults they confronted. Whether this would be true in day-to-day school activities remains to be seen, but the approach is certainly promising.

This is also an approach that might be used in teacher-training. Teachers, by and large, are as untrained as their students in stating their own positions, considering the options available to them, and then determining the consequences of their behavior. Neither teachers nor students are able to simulate different behavior and widen their repertoire of responses to a variety of situations; both still cling to the old rigidities of undefined self. Behavioral technology and appropriate curriculum can do a great deal to expand freedoms in the classroom.

ECOLOGICAL PRINCIPLES AND BEHAVIOR MODIFICATION

Other programs based on behavior-modification methods have also been successful in teaching children to adapt to their environment. Some of these programs have combined behavioral methods with ecological principles and a quest for the diffusion of power.

As examples, in two programs, groups of children in New York City—one from a residential treatment center and the other from a day school for delinquent children—were offered a unique reading program that proved quite successful in teaching academic skills.

The teachers enforced only two rules: pupils could not use physical force in the classroom, nor could they destroy property. The teachers informed the pupils that they would have to take over responsibility for their own learning. It was also stated to the children that while they might often have had teachers who seemed to confuse their roles with those of policemen, their present teachers would not. Instead, the teacher was there to answer any questions that came up, to correct work, and to guide the children through programmed materials in a way that made sense to the learners.

The teachers also explained that each pupil would be able to earn things he wanted—such as extra time playing basketball—for each correct answer in the programmed material, provided that 85 percent or more of the answers were correct on any given program. The teacher also provided a bonus for the *group* if *each* child could move up substantially in the reading program.

The utilization of a group is an effective solution to the problem of the anonymity of public schools, which to many children is a threat to their own group culture. Often delinquents who are successful in school according to school norms risk losing status outside school. And, of course, the peer group is the ultimate dispenser of rewards and punishments.

Some sociologists believe that school and academic learning are perceived as unmasculine by delinquents, and that the group is formed in order to have a masculine image that is at odds with the demands of the school. The same sociologists believe that this is particularly true in urban areas where it is much more common to find a female-centered household than it is in other areas of the country.

Despite this knowledge, schools continue to attempt to win individual students over to the traditional social values of success and reward, which are geared toward upward mobility. This attempt to win over individuals is sometimes called "the artichoke technique," because the teacher attempts to peel the child away from the group just as one might try to peel the leaves of an artichoke away from the stem. The technique seldom meets with success because of the limited rewards that are open to teachers and the relatively low power and status of the school when compared with that of the peer group.

Numerous studies have shown that great pressure is put on delinquent children *not* to conform to the rules of authority. Severe punishment is meted out by their peers to those children who *do* violate the code of the gang or group. In such cases, the group must consciously and explicitly legitimize learning so that individuals in the group need not concern themselves with loss of status for learning.

The success of the two New York City projects was probably based on the fact that the group took responsibility for itself, gave individual members permission to learn, and could concretely achieve its own goals and earn its own rewards.

The fact that the group took on the responsibility of managing itself is not unlike aspects of the civil-rights struggle in which groups and communities will manage themselves but will not be told what to do by others.

Usually there is little consonance between the world of the delinquent and the world of the school. Instead of being cognizant of the group and enlisting its support, and instead of utilizing their knowledge of groups and recognizing the legitimacy of such institutions as the gang, educators have traditionally ignored it. And this has been done at the expense of the teacher and the children.

The combination of reinforcement principles and ecological ways of looking at problems can also be used clinically. Adolescence is usually a period of great stress for parents as well as children. In one case, the principles of reinforcement theory were taught in a psychology course to an adolescent girl called Aimee. She then, on her own, began to apply them at home. Aimee felt that she was being scapegoated by her mother whenever her mother was in a bad mood. The girl's specific goals were to decelerate the number of fights and negative remarks that were made to her by her mother. Aimee eventually changed her mother's behavior, and her own as well, by reinforcing her mother's use of compliments and praise, while ignoring provocative and negative remarks. While there were still many times when fights did occur and tempers were lost, there was a significant change in the behavior of both parties.

In this case, it was not assumed that the parent, in her infinite wisdom, was the person who had to direct the behavior. It is not important who directs the behavior, as long as clashes between parties are minimized or healed. Also, children or adolescents are often more tractable than parents or teachers.

An important strength of the ecological model is that it doesn't concern itself with pathology: rather, it is involved with conflict without assuming that one of the parties in the conflict is "sick." The parties most concerned in the conflict can work directly on problems; no need exists for high-priced professionals to act as arbitrators, although it is very helpful to have professionals set up the mechanics of such programs.

If the mother and daughter have a problem, they can, given instruction in reinforcement methodology and the ability to control reinforcers for each other, work directly on their problem.

In the case of the children who changed their teacher's behavior, or the daughter who changed her mother's behavior, there was no need for psychologists to test the children or probe their psyche about their feelings toward their teacher or the mother. They knew their feelings too well! What they *did* lack beforehand was the technical knowledge and sophistication that would enable them to solve the problems themselves.

Paternalism and pathology do not have any significant role in the ecological approach. By definition, this approach trusts people to know what they want. It says that people are capable of making their own decisions and that children are people.

This does not mean that babies should be given matches and then left to themselves to decide whether to strike them or not. It *does* mean that if children are old enough to understand that they can control their own behavior—and have a significant effect on the lives of others—they can also begin to have a certain degree of decision-making and independence. They will undoubtedly make mistakes in how they come to their decisions; and some of their decisions will be foolish ones. But they may also learn to understand themselves better by having the freedom to perceive and correct their mistakes, and to gauge what effect they can have on their environment.

There will be times when children also try to use their power destructively, or to impose their will on others. They will then find that, in order to change behavior, they will have to control reinforcers, which will be inadequate in many instances; children will learn their own limitations, develop the ability to reach compromises, and find themselves growing toward a greater individual potential.

Children who have received instruction in this methodology will be in a better position to ensure that they receive what they need from others, and to perceive what others need from them. Hopefully, if enough students receive instruction in behavioral technology, the power of any one student—or teacher, too, for that matter—will be neutralized by that same knowledge in his peers or even in different age groupings.

It is important to stress here that we are dealing with behavioral technology and not with charismatic children or therapists of extraordinary skills and advanced training. The guidelines of reinforcement, in essence, are that:

1. A reinforcer is defined by its ability to accelerate or increase the rate at which any given behavior occurs.
2. Behavior that is not followed by reinforcement will decelerate or decrease in the frequency with which it occurs; this is not immediate, but gradual. At the same time that a behavior is ignored, it is advisable to increase the strength of another behavior, particularly a behavior that is incompatible with the unwanted behavior.
3. Reinforcers are idiosyncratic to individuals, and it is necessary to observe what functions as a reinforcer to the person(s) with whom one is working.
4. The best way to dispense reinforcers is to do so immediately after the desired behavior is emitted.
5. Reinforcement must be systematic and consistent to be effective.
6. When a desired behavior is not currently attainable, then reinforcing approximations to that behavior will eventually lead to the same result.

The above technology has met with strong resistance on the part of many school psychologists and clinical workers. They criticize the method as dehumanizing because, according to them, it views man as an animal who is fit only to be trained.

In reality, the method states that behavior is lawful and follows certain rules—in humans as well as in animals. When we know more about human behavior, we are in a better position to control it when the need is present. People are constantly shaping other people's behavior and having their own behavior shaped by other people. The results are often far from satisfactory and people engage in interactions that neither party desires.

A child who is labeled as "sick" or "retarded," or a "normal" child who is ill-treated by a teacher, can readily understand that *he* (the child) may not be the problem, but that he may be instrumental in the solution of the problem.

5

Programs That Can Make a Difference

Many kinds of programs can be instituted to ensure more adequate learning and the reduction of deviant behavior. Some of these approaches are discussed in this chapter. It is not intended that these programs should be accepted as panaceas, but merely as examples of what can be done.

For the most part, these programs break away from the rigidity of traditional education, and all can be implemented now without huge grants of revenue. In fact, most of these programs could be instituted tomorrow without increasing the cost of the school program at all. In many cases, the taxpayer would more than likely receive more value for his money than is currently the case.

Breaking away from the rigidity of traditional self-contained classrooms is an imperative for reducing "deviant" behavior within the schools. Individual differences between pupils can only be accommodated to a limited degree when there are one teacher, thirty pupils, and a set curriculum. Under traditional systems, the *rate* of learning becomes as important as learning itself, since group instruction is necessary in most classes. But if the rate of learning (as opposed to learning itself) is eliminated as an ultimate criterion, then the child who learns slowly is no longer retarded. Currently, departures from group norms become important criteria of deviance.

Through changes in the structure of the school, it is possible to establish programs that can accommodate a wide range of individual differences. When curriculum is individualized, each child can learn at his or her own rate. When a child is successfully involved in learning important skills he becomes too busy to engage in obstreperous behavior. Much deviant behavior is a result of placing a child under too much stress. Programs that individualize instruction lessen the amount of stress children face in classrooms.

The programs described in this chapter all emphasize procedures that allow individualization of instruction and/or allow the child a large voice in determining the consequences of his actions. Power and control are not as important in these programs as is learning. These programs can do a great deal for potential special-education children, as they allow these children to remain in the mainstream of education. There is little need in these programs to establish special classes, since every child is considered exceptional or in need of special instruction.

LEARNING CENTERS

Learning centers are an organized means of individualizing instruction for children in a classroom. Specifically, a learning center is an organizational arrangement that houses curriculum with behavioral objectives and different media, such as recordings, filmstrips, videotapes, cassette tapes, and books. Materials are related to a specific teaching unit in a specified area of the classroom. The teacher may have separate areas or small centers for social studies, mathematics, reading, drama, and so forth.

The learning center must house all the materials needed to accomplish these assignments, such as paper, pencils, books, tapes, recorders, filmstrips and viewers, crayons, and paint brushes. The children can use these resources themselves, just as they now use textbooks. Learning centers do not require a specific classroom arrangement, nor do they imply changes in architectural structure. They can be adapted to any architectural environment. Only the teachers' and students' imaginations can limit them.

Darrell Mattoon, principal of Mineral King School in Visalia, California, reports that the school's Learning Centers Program has reduced the number of deviant children in the fourth, fifth, and sixth grades.

To place students in learning centers, they are given criteria tests in subject-matter areas to determine at what level they are functioning. If they are not on grade level in reading, math, spelling, and penmanship, it is recommended that at least the first three hours of the school day should be devoted to special-skill subjects. After the passing of criteria tests, children should be permitted to play a larger role in pursuing subjects that interest them.

During either class or independent time, the students go to one of the centers and work in pairs or in small groups. Materials are on different reading levels and are organized in a sequential manner so that the student can go from the easiest to the most difficult task in the center. In one school, C.S. 77 in the Bronx, New York, enterprising teachers transcribed social-studies texts onto cassette tapes so that even nonreaders could participate in the program.

Students are also encouraged to prepare their own materials and to develop their own ideas for learning centers. The criteria for all curricula should adhere to the standard set by the Follow Through Program, described in chapter 3. Materials and equipment can be arranged so that the teacher can work with small groups or on an individual basis. Because of the active involvement of the children, teachers should expect noise, movement, and discussion by the children. Each teacher and class have their own level of noise tolerance. The noise level needs to be decided by discussion among the teacher and students.

The teacher can redesign the classroom to buffer noise. Some new classrooms have carpets and acoustical ceilings, but, lacking these, small rugs or carpeted areas will help. Putting cloth over bare surfaces and the use of pillows in some areas is very effective, and if drapes are used in the room, they could be drawn to serve as noise softeners. Portable bulletin-board barriers made of textured wallboard can be used to separate the center visually and can also reduce noise. In fact, the use of any soft material to break up an open-space classroom is very effective in reducing noise.

When starting learning centers, teachers can have the children rehearse moving from one center to another on a distinctive signal, such as turning off the lights or sounding a bell. The centers are lined up so that movement is easy and orderly. Contingencies can be applied to facilitate children's learning these routines.

The teacher has to make sure that the materials will make instruction motivating and interesting. The children working at these stations can be encouraged to attack the materials as a team and thus encourage socially adaptive behavior. Ideas and tasks are placed at each station for students. The students determine what the directions mean, what is to be done, and how they can best complete the assignment. The assigned tasks may be specific, or allow the students a number of options, or be completely open-ended. This can be determined by the teacher and students.

Five to eight learning centers or stations are recommended for each class. They should be placed far enough from each other so that the children can move from one center to another with a minimum of noise and activity. Children can be assigned to stations in groups and are rotated each day or by period, depending on class choice.

Most teachers organize their stations according to purpose. These centers incorporate as much student selection as the class is able to handle. The centers usually utilize the following schemes:

1. Stations may be developed around traditional subject matter, such as arithmetic, reading, science, spelling, social studies, and music.
2. Learning centers may be constructed around one subject, with stations subdivided according to different aspects of this subject. For example, a learning center for English could have different stations for creative writing, grammar, English usage, spelling, storytelling, story writing, poetry, and report writing.
3. Special stations, such as a bonus station, can be provided by the teacher for students who have completed work or earned extra bonus points. A bonus station can be a place where a child may go to select a project with great interest for him. The bonus station is also used as a reward for children who have done work well and their reward—instead of money, M & M's, or material rewards—is the privilege of choosing an activity at the bonus station.
4. In a conference station the teacher conducts evaluative con-

ferences with students. Children can also use this station to hold a conference with another student, to work with the teacher in a project, or just talk on a one-to-one basis with the teacher. Either the child or the teacher can initiate this conference.

5. A help station is where children can come for specific help on any one of their assignments. The assistance may come from another student or from the teacher. It is best to organize a room in such a manner that at least part of the assistance provided in the help station will be from peers.

6. A thought station is where a child goes to read a book, look out the window, do nothing, or, as one small child said, "To take my coffee break that I earned for doing my other work." Generally, children have to earn the right to go to the thought station by completing assignments, following directions, and doing other tasks in other stations or at their seat. The thought station is merely another form of bonus station that provides a child with a quiet reflective place he can go to after completing other classroom work.

There are certain disadvantages to the use of learning centers. They require a great deal of teacher planning if they are to be more than depositories of gimmicky materials, and curriculum objectives have to be made quite explicit. But in the authors' opinion, the advantages far outweigh the disadvantages. For one thing, students themselves can receive a good education by working with their teachers in specifying behavioral objectives for subject-matter areas, and this kind of program can evolve slowly rather than having a class move immediately from one form of instruction to another. In addition, there will be many more curriculum options open to pupils using this system, and children can have the opportunity to explore many interests and become proficient in a few.

In a learning center there are also fewer restrictions on movement and noise than there are in traditional classrooms, and there is more opportunity for individuals to learn what *they* need instead of the traditional approach of the teacher working with the average student, who exists only in statistics.

This type of program has been used in many school districts, and the majority of them report a reduction in referrals to special education as a result of the program. Wide ranges in achievement are expected and can be dealt with accordingly.

INDIVIDUALLY GUIDED EDUCATION

Individually Guided Education (IGE) is a means of combining learning centers and team teaching. IGE is an administrative structure that can facilitate accountability and break down the walls of the classroom. Rules are generally made by those who have to live with them, and students, teachers, and parents can have a greater say in what goes on in their lives.

The teachers of Baxley School in Nebraska, including the special-class teacher, became a team in planning and implementing an IGE program. The special-class teacher became the resource person and the consultant in aiding the other teachers prepare techniques for individualized work for slow learners. During the previous summer, in preparation for the implementation of the program, the teachers spent three weeks preparing learning centers for social studies, science, reading, math, and language. The teachers wrote their own placement tests, to be administered to all students before the children were grouped in reading and math sections. The staff then divided itself into four groups. The teachers agreed they would all teach reading at the same time every day and the children would move from group to group instead of having the teachers move. The first week of school was spent administering the placement tests in reading and math. All of the children in the fourth, fifth, and sixth grades were placed according to the scores obtained in their math and reading tests. The special-education teacher and his aide worked as regular teachers, using the special-education room as their headquarters. Each had twelve students in his reading group, and of the total of twenty-four students only four had previously been in a special-education room. Each teacher in the program wrote out behavioral objectives for each student in math and reading.

During the summer the teachers had also written continuous-progress tests that would be used to test each student every four weeks. After each test, the groups were reshuffled so that students could be moved ahead or recycled to materials that they had not adequately learned. Teachers kept records on the rate of progress for all children. All of this information was graphed, giving the teachers on the team a means of evaluating the daily progress of each child.

The first two hours of each morning were spent in reading and math. Then the children rotated to different learning centers. The children were allowed to select centers in social studies, science, foreign language, or arts and crafts. Each student was allowed to select two centers from a list of sixteen available.

A great deal of research from industrial psychology has concluded that, when people have the opportunity to complete tasks in their own way, they receive more self-satisfaction, have more interest in their tasks, and do more efficient work as well. IGE is decentralized and places decisions in the hands of the learners and teachers; at the same time it brings in a great deal of accountability.

Schools taking part in the IGE program are converted from traditional grade levels to a multiunit organizational pattern. Each unit has a professional staff of two to six teachers, one or more teacher aides, and 50 to 150 children of varying age range. There may be a two- or three-year age range of children in the unit, with pupils grouping and regrouping as they pursue different learning objectives.

IGE schools operate with an Instructional Improvement Committee (IIC) composed of the principal and unit leaders. The IIC reviews educational policies to ensure that the separate units reinforce each other's work as each youngster moves up the age ladder. The multiunit structure and the IIC are the primary means by which self-improvement takes place within an IGE school.

Instructional processes represent the heart of IGE. Those processes provide each student with appropriate learning programs built on a continuous cycle of finding out where each student is and how he got there (assessment), deciding what he needs to learn next (specifying objectives), selecting the ways for him to obtain those objectives (diversified learning opportunities), and making sure that he has met them (reassessment).

How each student fits into the program is determined by an assessment the teacher and pupil make of the learner's achievements, aptitude, and learning styles as they relate to learning objectives. Children may be placed for varying time spans into one of four basic learning modes:

1. INDEPENDENT. The student works more or less alone at his own rate. This may involve simply reading a book in the classroom or in the library, or working with various printed resource materials or with audio tapes or films. When the student needs help from the teacher he is free to get it.
2. ONE-TO-ONE STUDY. This means access to tutoring, from either the teacher, a teacher aide, or another student. It is

often essential for remedial work, and for oral work such as giving of reports. Planning and assessment conferences are also held on a one-to-one basis.

3. SMALL GROUP. IGE's developers see the small group as the key to the program. Each group consists of from four to eleven students working to achieve a common learning objective. The group may be teacher-led, student-led with a teacher present, or student-led without a teacher present. Groups stay together as long as the teacher and the group feel is necessary for the immediate tasks, which include functioning as a tutorial unit, as a discussion group, or a place to plan a project, or accomplishing some other specific task.

4. LARGE GROUP. A group of thirty-five pupils or the entire unit may be brought together on occasion. The purpose may be to hear a guest speaker, or to see a special film or show or program by an outside group or by one of the other units.

The cost of implementing an IGE program depends largely on the investment a school district wishes to make. Some schools draw more heavily on volunteers than upon paid clerical and instructional aides. Schools adapt existing curriculum materials to IGE.

School facilities need not be a barrier to IGE. The program is in operation in both "egg-crate" and "open-plan" schools. Some school buildings housing IGE programs were constructed around the turn of the century.

Preliminary evidence from a Wisconsin center's early implementation of the multiunit school and incorporation of the curriculum component in reading indicated dramatic increases in student achievement over a short period of time. A report of *Professional Satisfaction on Decision Making in the Multiunit School* by Roland J. Pellegrin, a professor of sociology at the University of Oregon, disclosed a high rate of professional satisfaction in the multiunit school. Pellegrin stated that "we have evidence that group participation in decision making is highly regarded by faculty members of multiunit schools. In interviews, high job satisfaction and increased effectiveness were attributed to teacher involvement in the decisions affecting their work."

COOPERATIVE TEACHING

Cooperative teaching can also be used to facilitate learning and reduce educational casualties. Cooperative teaching is any method whereby a teacher utilizes one or more students as an active part of the teaching process.

It has been well documented that many children (some estimates are as high as 20 percent) fail to master basic reading skills. Often teachers can easily identify the students' needs, but the teacher cannot individualize instruction sufficiently to help them. If we decide to rely on the reading specialist, the psychologist, or other outside personnel to work individually with each hampered pupil, we will find it necessary to wait long into the twenty-first century before our manpower shortage is ended. But of course by this time the original nonreading student will have grown to adulthood, and if he did not learn to read on his own, it will be far too late to alleviate his deficiency.

This projection is not idle guesswork but is based on a series of demographic studies conducted by the Bureau for the Education of the Handicapped when Dr. James Gallagher was its commissioner. One very effective way of dealing with the manpower crisis is to enlist students in team learning programs. Dr. Gerard A. Poirier encourages teachers to divide their classrooms systematically into learning teams. Poirier states: "The main objective of team learning is respect for the uniqueness of the person." He describes a classroom where the students are no longer facing the teacher. Instead, two halves of the class face each other. These two halves are further divided into units of four to six students. The teacher works with classroom units rather than each student individually.

In Poirier's plan, each unit of students has a co-leader and at least four other members. The leader and the co-leader switch roles and help to organize and assist the group. The most successful method that Poirier found in selecting a leader was through the teacher's judgment based upon knowledge of the student's academic and social behavior. Students are grouped heterogeneously in academic subjects, but the teacher selects students who can function effectively as a team.

In a discussion of classroom ecology a sociology professor once stated that "those in the front rows are working for A's; those in the middle of the room are playing it safe and will settle for B's and C's; and those in the back rows are the rebels." Whereupon one of the back-row boys responded, "Oh, no, Professor, that's not correct. I'm just here so I can get out of the class sooner."

"You see what I mean?" asked the professor. "By dividing the class into teams there are no back rows, front rows, or middle rows. The entire classroom is grouped together into teams, which are moved at least six times during the year to obviate any one team securing a favored position. In addition, the teacher may shift a team member if irreconcilable differences prevent effective functioning."

In team learning, the teacher's role becomes managerial and facilitative, since he must not only organize students and skills but must assist in helping each group meet its objectives. The teams and team leaders participate more in decision-making roles than in a traditional classroom. Since students are grouped in teams, they provide instruction for each other in solving the problems presented to them. Often direct instruction by the teacher is not required or desired by students. They request assistance from the teacher when necessary. The teacher is then free to assist in the planning and evaluation of student progress. In team learning, the class is student-oriented rather than teacher-dominated. Students slowly move toward the center of the stage and play a more active role in guiding their own learning.

CROSS-AGE TUTORING—COOPERATIVE TEACHING. Cross-age tutoring is a dynamic teaching process where older students, with the guidance of teachers, are trained to help younger students with their learning problems, either on a one-to-one tutorial basis, or by assisting small groups of students. Cross-age tutoring is a program that uses the educational resources inherent in the school population by developing responsibility among older tutors to assist younger children in subject areas and interpersonal relationships. In some cases, extremely competent young children can also provide assistance for students.

Tim Murphy was a seventh-grader in Delta School, Jackson, Louisiana. He was the brightest student in the entire district. When his intelligence was first tested in the fourth grade, it was at the near-genius level. Tim's father had been an oil worker most of his life. Tim was a late arrival, being born when his mother and father were both in their late forties. Most of Tim's childhood had been spent around adults. Tim just didn't act like a child. This created few problems for Tim until he was an adolescent. Then the other students started teasing him about the way he acted.

Tim did not know how to react to the teasing. First he sulked, and then he grew quite aggressive. He rapidly became a severe disciplinary problem at school.

Tim was in a two-period social-studies class for men-tally gifted minors. The teacher spent one quarter of the term teaching his students learning theory, how to write behavioral objectives, reinforcement procedures and pro-gramming. The students had to use these skills with peers at school and were then sent to a kindergarten-to-sixth-grade school as tutors.

Tim was one of the most apt pupils in the class. The teacher held additional sessions with him to explain how he could use behavior modification with peers when they teased him. After the quarter was over, Tim went with the rest of the class to work as a peer tutor. Tim was an instant success. He was able to devise learning and behav-ioral strategies for his own pupils and helped others solve problems with the students they were tutoring.

Tim's knowledge and ability in applying behavior modification with peers and his success in tutoring gave him the skill and confidence needed to solve his own conflicts with his peers. He became one of the most popu-lar students in his class, and his peers looked to him for assistance rather than as a target for teasing.

An excellent cross-age tutoring project was designed by Robert Hall, a junior high school teacher at Divisadero School, Visalia, California. Hall needed no additional equipment or materials for training his tutors. He used students in his seventh- and eighth-grade core classes, who were interested in cross-age tutoring. They received in-tensive training in daily two-hour sessions for six weeks. This training consisted of the principles and practices of reinforcement theory, learning how to write behavioral objectives, and tutoring skills. The students attended daily classes and learned basic behavior-modification methodology, in much the same way as college students do before practice teaching. They also divided up and practiced techniques on each other, teaching sample lessons that would normally be presented to fourth-, fifth-, and sixth-grade children.

After demonstrating their competency, trainees were matched (by Hall and fourth-, fifth-, and sixth-grade teachers at Royal Oaks School) with target students who were selected because of special tutoring needs. The seventh- and eighth-grade students tutored the fourth-, fifth-, and sixth-graders for a six-week period, two hours daily. In addition, they met as a class on Mondays with their teacher to discuss their progress or problems. Videotape was used extensively in the training session so the tutorial students could get actual counts on their positive statements and could also practice and rehearse techniques for positive verbal reinforcement. Many of the tutors used token economies and other reinforcement systems with their target students.

One of the most interesting developments of the project was the realization by the tutors that they were in fact becoming teachers. They commented that the Monday meetings seemed like teachers' meetings. The materials used in the tutoring session were used in the regular classroom and were provided by the teacher of the target students. Two weeks before the tutoring started, the tutors met twice weekly after school to familiarize themselves with the materials.

The tutoring program proved to be extremely successful and is now in its second year. The program has the enthusiastic support of teachers, tutors, and target students. A unique factor of the program was that no additional funding was needed to get it started.

An American educator who recently visited China noted that, owing to the limited finances available, Chinese schools and nurseries have very few toys and almost no teaching machines or hardware. The effect on the children is that they are forced to relate to each other for entertainment and motivation. The American educator noted that quite often in American schools, students spend more time relating to equipment, machinery, and books than they do to each other. Curriculum does need to be individualized, but students should be encouraged to work in twos, threes, or even larger groups. We do not want a school system that encourages individualization and at the same time impedes social consciousness. Student team teaching, cross-age tutoring, and peer tutoring are a means to develop sociability in children.

Cross-age tutoring provides a similar social relationship to that of the one-room schoolhouse where students assisted in tutoring other students in their own classroom. In the schools of the 1880s and 1890s, cross-age tutoring was natural, since there was generally one classroom with children from first grade through high school sharing the same room. In today's schools, which are segregated by grade, older students seldom have the opportunity for social interchange with younger children. In schools separated by grade, younger and older students are often in conflict regarding playground space, balls and equipment, seats on the bus, and places in line at the school cafeteria. Cross-age tutoring provides an opportunity for older students to become aware of younger children as persons with individual problems.

Through cross-age tutoring, older students learn to share the feelings, ideas, problems, successes, and failures of younger children. The realization by an older student that he can help another child and the importance of being a teacher to those younger than himself can engender feelings of dignity and worth much akin to that felt by adult teachers.

The following example illustrates how a cooperative teaching program can resolve student problems. Ann Wyrick had taught the sixth grade in a semirural Iowa community for seven years. She had always been a non-authoritarian teacher, who relied a great deal on her relationship with individuals and with the class.

When the school year started in September, Ann divided the entire class into groups of four to six students. Each group selected a leader and co-leader for a two-month period.

The class loved the team learning. The room was constantly a buzz of children helping each other with their assignments. The class became very close. The team learning had a very cohesive effect upon most of the students. It also gave Ann more time for planning and a greater freedom to work with students who had special problems.

She used continuous-progress tests with the children to make sure they were learning the subject matter they were studying. She involved the team leaders in grading papers and planning learning strategies for their groups. The result was that the class no longer had one teacher—it had thirty teachers cooperating together!

The best illustration of the effectiveness of the project on human relations in the class was Sally. Sally McKendrick transferred to the class in the middle of January. She was a very small, redheaded, freckle-faced girl. At first Ann thought Sally was very shy and quiet, until her third day in class, when she kicked one of the boys in her team until he was black and blue. The incident happened on the playground, and the other students said that she also used obscene language. When Sally came to the teacher she was already in tears. Sally continued to be a serious problem in class and on the playground.

Ann Wyrick met with the leader and co-leader of Sally's group and asked them to help Sally and to stick up for her when she needed help. Sally's team really took up her cause, and soon the rest of the class did, too. Ann had the team walk away from Sally when she had an outburst and they encouraged others around her to do the same. They didn't talk to her about the outburst and they didn't respond when she had a temper tantrum.

The teacher kept track of the frequency of the outbursts. During the week after the conference with Sally, Sally had twelve temper tantrums, the next week she had ten, but on the third week after being ignored, she had only four. After six weeks Sally stopped having temper tantrums completely.

The team kept on working with Sally and she became a contributing member of her team. When the next quarter was over and the class elected new team leaders and co-leaders, Sally was chosen as co-leader of her group. Ann Wyrick made a home call and told Sally's mother about the progress she had made at school. Sally's mother was very pleased and commented that this was the first school Sally had liked since she had been in the second grade.

Sally wasn't the best student in class and still had an occasional temper flareup. But she was a cooperative, successful member of her team and a contributing member of the class. All of Sally's problems were not solved by any means, but she became a successful student.

CLASSROOM MEETINGS

Another type of program for reducing deviant behavior in the classroom that deserves consideration is the classroom meeting. This program has been derived from the work of Dr. William Glasser and can be implemented immediately in virtually any classroom. Glasser's techniques do not require extensive administrative support and planning.

Due to the fact that Glasser has not successfully defined the objectives of the classroom meetings, it is difficult to evaluate the effectiveness of the program, but most reports indicate that problems of social deviancy can be handled quite effectively with this program, since there are shared expectancies of social behavior.

The cornerstone to Glasser's reality therapy and to his program in *Schools Without Failure* can be stated in one word—commitment. When a child or a teacher makes a commitment to change behavior, no excuse is acceptable for not following through. Students and teacher alike are held responsible for their voluntary commitments to change. This puts the entire class on an accountability basis. The teacher is accountable to students, students to teacher, and each to self. In this way, students learn to make decisions about changing their social behavior or academic skills, and then they will be expected to fulfill such commitments, or to change the goals if they are unable to reach them.

Glasser's techniques and philosophy can do much to involve students in their own education and teach them to assume responsibility for their own lives. While there is little evidence that his techniques reduce the cost of education or enhance academic achievement, these techniques can do a great deal to promote student and teacher satisfaction. Problems common to teachers and pupils can be worked on together and joint solutions can be worked out that are satisfactory to all persons involved in the transaction. Power is shared.

There are three basic kinds of classroom meetings recommended in the Glasser program. The class meeting most germane to reducing deviant behavior is the social-problem-solving meeting. During a class meeting, the problem under consideration is discussed by the students and teacher. In reality therapy (a term Glasser uses) this is called exposing the problem for open, honest discussion. After a discussion of the problem, the teacher then begins pressing the class for a solution. The class meeting is followed up with progress meetings where the implementation of the steps taken to resolve the problem is evaluated, and new strategies and steps are agreed upon.

In social-problem-solving class meetings the teacher listens to the reasons given by students for stealing, poor school attendance, or for fighting—whatever the problem—and whenever students provide a valid reason the teacher must consider changing his techniques so the school program will become more worthwhile to the students. In this format, the students enter into the discussion, determine some of the problems they would like to see solved, and commit themselves to solving them.

The following case study is an example of how the use of the class meeting improved an immediate problem and had a positive effect on the relationships between students, teachers, and administration.

Sam Williams taught eighth-grade civics and had two periods of counseling in Meridian, Mississippi. Most of the teachers and students in the school were black. Bill, one of the students in Sam Williams's civics class, frequently cut school on warm days during the spring and fall to go swimming or fishing. Whenever possible, he would take some of the other boys with him. The principal was very concerned and told Williams that if the truancy did not stop, he would have to file a complaint with the district attorney that the boys were out-of-control minors. Sam Williams decided to try class meetings as a means of getting the problem out in the open.

Sam started the first meeting by asking the class if all of them were present that day. A few of the boys snickered, and one said, "Man, you know we not all here." This eventually developed into a discussion, timid at first on the part of some, but shortly more frank and open.

The students admitted they knew eight students were absent, and that those absent were cutting school.

The next thing Sam did was to ask some of those present if they also frequently skipped class, and many admitted they did. At this point the students knew that Sam did not intend to punish them and that he was merely inquiring why they missed class. Finally Sam asked them what they thought would happen to them when they went to high school if their same pattern of cutting school continued. Some of the students said they thought they would probably be suspended or maybe sent to the courts. All of the students admitted they would probably not attend high school any more regularly than they were currently attending junior high school.

At that point, Sam determined it was time to stop this particular discussion. They had gone as far in one session as he wanted to go. An open, honest relationship had been reached between the students and himself. All of them were telling the truth and dealing with each other and the problems that they faced in an honest manner. The discussion was then terminated.

Later, discussions were held and the students formulated a number of ways to deal with the problem. The teacher received written contracts from six of the boys. These contracts stipulated the changes the boys would make in attendance patterns. The contracts were written in clear, concise, behavioral terms. Five of the six boys fulfilled their contracts.

THE VOUCHER PLAN

This program requires extensive community and administrative support and can change education directly.

The voucher plan, where every parent would receive

public money to spend at the school of his choice, is coming under more frequent discussion. The use of vouchers would bring competition into education, and those schools which did not satisfy the needs or desires of parents would simply not be able to operate; at the very least, schools would have to offer services to children that parents felt were worth investing in. In its purest form, the voucher system would be open to private and parochial schools as well as public schools.

Christopher Jencks and his colleagues at Harvard University have concluded that schools *per se* make very little difference in the life chances of individual children. Personality characteristics and random factors or luck were more important than the type of schooling received when it came to financial success as an adult. Jencks and his colleagues concluded that teachers do not know much more than parents or children when it comes to the ideal form of schooling. Thus he felt a major criterion for schooling should be that it satisfy the desires of parents and children, and teachers should derive satisfaction from the place where they work.

The voucher plan permits parents and children to have a significant voice in the kind of education desired. Teachers, too, would be happier under this plan, since there would be a variety of educational programs offered and they would have a wider variety of schools to choose from.

One of the first school districts to operate under the voucher plan was in San Jose, California. Contrary to the fears of civil-rights groups and liberals, the voucher plan did not polarize the community into ethnic groupings or into schools for rich and schools for poor. This might have been because private schools were excluded from the plan and parents could not supplement the basic voucher fund. In addition, each school had to admit any applicant who applied. Teachers' unions have been opposed to the voucher plan, perhaps fearing parents would have too large a voice in what schools offered, and many other people feared that a voucher plan would lead to racial polarization. But the situation at San Jose seemed to have been particularly harmonious.

Most parents opted for the traditional offerings in traditional classrooms, but there were other kinds of schools that attracted support. These included schools that stressed the arts and a school that taught all subjects through a core curriculum with a stress on skills needed for daily living—for example, mathematics was taught through shopping and crafts activities, etc. Other schools stressed ethnic identification, and one school stressed preparing for the future by teaching subjects such as ecology.

One principal reported that "unexcused absences are down, vandalism is down, and the kids obviously feel better about school. They've done at least as well as they would have done normally, and next year they'll do even better—the whole thing will come together. The teachers have worked far and above what they did before. They're tired, but they're pleased with themselves."

Achievement data are not in yet on this project, but all apparent results are that the program is a success. At the very least, there has been a big boost in morale in the school district, and there is an enthusiasm about education that is often lacking in the public schools.

This is a program that must be instituted by the school board of a community working in close collaboration with teacher and parent groups. It does not require more money to run a school program this way. In fact, with competition introduced, and accountability a very real part of the program, there is likely to be considerably less waste and more emphasis on providing quality services. After all, stores that keep on offering shoddy merchandise and have incompetent employees usually go out of business. With this kind of incentive, there is likely to be an improvement in the goods and services offered. At the very least, people will be able to make meaningful choices and will themselves be responsible for the kind of education offered to their children. And, most important, power will be shared, so that people can have something to say about how their lives are to be affected. Instances of deviancy will also decrease, since it will be possible to find a program that melds with the behavior of the individual.

THE FREE SCHOOLS

Of the 10 percent of American children who do not attend schools within the public system, the most rapid student population growth in the past few years has been in those programs called "free schools," "alternative schools," "open schools," "new schools," or similar-sounding names. Such terminology generally describes a private school that is based on principles of student self-motivation and self-direction and the importance of personal development for each student. Such schools tend to maximize the students' opportunity to determine curricula by virtually eliminating controls on the students. The free school concept, then, is that only the learner can judge the effects of the learning process.

The free schools represent a growing influence in our educational system. To start anything so complex as a school is an enormously complicated and difficult matter, and the mere fact that so many teachers, parents, and students have been willing to make such a commitment of time, energy, and interest is testimony to the need for such schools.

It should be noted, however, that in the free-school movement power is almost always seen in negative terms by teachers and staff. Thus one of the basic problems of the free-school movement becomes a pervasive fear of structure and power, with the result that those who are ostensibly to be in control of the educational situation usually end up by acting and by being perceived as intellectually neutral. Rigorous instruction or holding children responsible for high levels of accomplishment is lacking, and there is usually a great reluctance to evaluate work, which even extends to a similar reluctance on the part of pupils to show their work to either peers or teachers.

Jonathan Kozol, one of the founders of the free-school movement, recently stated that their "fear of power places a premium on mediocrity, nonvital leadership, insipid character, and unremarkable life-style. An organization, of whatever kind, that identifies real excellence or effectiveness with the terrifying risk of authoritarian manipulation will drive away all interesting and brilliant people and will establish in their stead norms of communal mediocrity."

While the free schools have many problems, they have in many cases been quite successful with students who were deviant, i.e., students who became "failures" by not meeting the expectations of those who held power over them in programs that would not deviate from the *status quo*. For example, Susie R. had mediocre grades in tenth grade, had failed art and English, and was a familiar face in the detention hall of the public high school she attended. School was an extremely unpleasant place for her. Many of her teachers actively disliked her. The only thing about school that Susie really enjoyed was meeting her friends during study hall, cutting class, and smoking marijuana between classes. Outside of school, however, Susie was a different person. She picked up enough money to travel to Mexico by selling her art work, was very successful in tutoring younger children, and enjoyed reading, interacting with people, and camping.

After one particularly unpleasant altercation with her English teacher, Susie left school and enrolled in a free school in an urban area. She was surprised at the amount of work that was entailed in operating a free school. Painting, janitorial work, and procuring supplies were all chores that had to be performed by the students. Susie felt that she had a stake in the school and did these jobs. In many cases she had to find her own teachers as well. The students did this by posting notices around the city, asking for part-time teachers who would volunteer their services. They were quite successful in finding teachers who wanted to share their skills. Susie floundered about in many subjects but was quite successful in art and English. She studied art because she enjoyed it and she wanted to be an art teacher. Her teacher did not have any academic credentials but was a successful commercial artist, and Susie learned many skills and received a great deal of encouragement to pursue art. She studied English because she recognized her own deficiencies and felt that her new English teacher taught skills instead of abstractions.

She did moderately well in her other subjects and used one of her old classmates as her math teacher. After two years in the free school Susie was accepted into a state university. She was accepted because of the quality of her portfolio and because the admissions officers were impressed with her initiative and her ability to formulate goals for herself. They were also impressed with her perseverance in meeting these goals. The free-school personnel and the college teachers were not concerned with her "deviant" behavior because outside of the public high school she was not perceived in that manner.

The "failure" of bright and creative students within public schools has been well documented. Some progressive school systems have begun to adapt ideas from the free schools into their own operations. In one suburban Westchester, New York, school system, administrators and teachers as well as parents were concerned with the apathy that many of the students felt, the declining attendance rates, and the failure of very capable young men and women. They created a "school within a school" and modeled it after a free school. The rest of the high school was run on a traditional basis. Students in the free school were given a large voice in what and how they should study. Formal academic courses were held, but the school also allowed students to work out apprenticeships with practicing artists, researchers, schools for the handicapped, and businessmen and mechanics.

Students also had to participate in the nitty-gritty operations of making a school run. They were involved in the decision-making to some degree and also in the responsibilities of ordering, answering the phone, planning a budget, improving the effectiveness of the operation, and so on.

As a result of the school within a school, there has been increased attendance, and a higher percentage of students now finish high school. The majority of the students in the school within a school are no longer perceived as school failures, as they are meeting the expectations of their teachers and their own expectations as well.

Urban schools have also begun schools within schools. Some urban schools house thousands of students. Out of administrative "necessity" pupils are reduced to numbers instead of individuals. By creating schools within schools it has become possible to deal with children as individuals. As ecological psychologists would predict, there appears to be greater student and faculty participation in academic and nonacademic activities within these small schools, and consequently less deviancy.

This trend has not been a panacea. Some students still drift around, goalless and confused, and the teaching staff has not been able to meet the needs of many students. But they are doing a better job than was formerly done, and many students have fared extremely well in the open-school format. In addition, many surrounding school systems have begun to copy this model. Even within the traditional sections of the high schools, teachers are working with their students to formulate goals together and students are gaining increasing respect from their teachers and administrators.

6

Special Education Can
Be Special

Even in the most individualized educational programs there are children who require and can benefit from special-class placement. This is particularly true of the severely retarded child, or those so physically maimed or psychologically aberrant that they have little or no chance of participating in regular school programs. But for the majority of pupils in special-education classes their placement there has been far too easy a way for educators to solve their difficulties with children who do not "learn" quickly and efficiently, or who defy rules and get into personality conflicts with their teachers. These children may be quite difficult to work with, but they do not necessarily need special education as it is currently practiced.

School officials think that problems are over when the child has been labeled as having "learning disabilities," but an equally valid procedure would be to label the teacher as having "teaching disabilities."

One current danger of special-education programs is that they can absolve the teacher from the responsibility of devising new methods to teach children who do not easily learn skills. Another danger is that these programs decrease the tolerance of parents, educators, and students for the child who deviates from the norm.

Special-education classes are also criticized because of cost. Virtually all of them have a lower pupil-teacher ratio than regular classes. They often have special and expensive curricula and large staffs. Transportation is also a major cost, and pupils are often taken away from their own communities and placed in a special facility.

THE NEED FOR SPECIAL EDUCATION

There are many problems concerning special education. While special education is *not* a sinister plot to keep certain children in an inferior status, most tests of achievement, intelligence, and personality have serious shortcomings. They are not functional in telling teachers what to do with the child once his or her score is known. Test results should always be countered with these crucial questions put to the testor: "So what?" and "What do I do now?" In addition, testors should never be allowed to say, "Be warm and supportive and give him individual attention," when warm and supportive are not spelled out specifically and the logistics of the teaching situation preclude individual tutoring.

Many liberal critics are quick to condemn these tests, but these critics ignore the host of studies (few of which have been satisfactorily refuted) documenting that these instruments, for all their shortcomings, do have a respectable predictive validity: the child who scores 70 on an individual IQ test will encounter difficulty in mastering school requirements. The child will have this difficulty whether he has been tested or not tested—or whether he has been labeled or not labeled.

Labels might contribute to problems, but a label is earned by behavior that is getting the child into trouble in the first place. In fact, as former Assistant U.S. Commissioner of Education Dr. James Gallagher has pointed out, the whole labeling controversy is in many ways naïve. Some people think that a problem is solved, or at least understood, when a label is affixed; other people, equally naïve, think the problem will disappear if there is no label to call attention to it. Both viewpoints miss the central issue that the label is brought into being *because* there is a violation of expectancies, and a fixed curriculum and school structure that do not accommodate individual differences. The question of what kind of standards should be used to judge pupils and what kinds of educational programs will be most beneficial are the central questions. Both decisions, to label or not to label, might be bad; but some attention to the problem is unavoidable.

Gallagher has pointed out that there are positive aspects to labeling and to special education. For example, Dr. Frank Hewett of the University of California at Los Angeles has succeeded in creating engineered classrooms where pupils receive enough of an academic boost to remain in general education. Using special-education methods, autistic children have been taught how to speak and read and to interact with their peers and teachers. The Re-Ed project in Tennessee has been remarkably successful in setting up residential centers where the focus is in reducing child-family-school strife. Re-Ed has taught children how to live in groups and to take responsibility for their own behavior, as well as teaching them academic skills. At the same time, Re-Ed staff have increased the tolerance of the school and community for different behavior.

Polemics in education, and especially the argument that special education must be dismantled in its entirety, can be harmful to children. For one thing, some children do have special needs, and it would be naïve to think that money earmarked for general education would trickle down to those with special needs. Legislators do not and should not disburse money proportionately. Secondly, a cadre of researchers, teaching personnel, and a rich teaching methodology and curriculum have been built around categories and labels. It would be foolish to disband what resources have been built up, only to find that we would have to begin again to help those with special needs. In many respects special education can be a positive force for children's growth and can provide a model for general education. Special education can be in the forefront of curriculum development, teaching methodology, and utilization of personnel. The methodologies and practices of selected special-education programs can be extrapolated to general education for the well-being of all students, not just a selected few. The question then becomes, what can be taken from special education?

CONTRACTS IN EDUCATION

Gallagher has suggested one approach toward accountability within special education that could be generalized to school systems.

In essence, his suggestions are that the placement of any perceived primary-school-aged exceptional child into a special-education unit should require a written contract, signed by both responsible school officials and parents. (It would be desirable to have children at the intermediate level and above be a party to the contract.) Gallagher

talks about those who are perceived as moderately handicapped, and not the trainable mentally retarded child
or the psychotic youngster. The contract should contain
specific goals as to what reading or arithmetic level the
child will reach, or by what percentage the number of
temper tantrums or other negative behaviors will decrease. The contract should also contain a specific time
limit. The time limit would counteract the fact that children placed in special-education units often remain there
throughout their school careers. Because children remaining in regular classes usually learn more than special-education students (even though the IQ is the same),
with a resulting disparity between the two groups increasing rather than decreasing, Gallagher suggests that this
contract be *nonrenewable:* if the contract is to be renewed
it should be done only after some type of quasi-judicial
hearing where the parents and the child are represented
by a legal or a child-advocate counsel. The contract would
be made by the school system only after a lengthy educational diagnosis, which would commit the school to working toward measurable educational objectives. The contract could be upgraded every six months.

Gallagher has pointed out that such a contract would
have obvious advantages from the parent's and child's
point of view, but he also states it would be equally helpful to educators. Educators would have a clear and measurable set of objectives to work toward. Special-education administrators could have a bargaining point within
the school system for more resources if it could be documented that existing resources were inadequate.

One of the objectives that most parents would insist
upon would be reintegration of their special child into
the regular-education track. This would compel regular
educators to take part in the contract negotiations and
signing, and to work with the special educators to fit the

child back into the system—even if that means that the system had to be changed. Right now special and general education each have their own bureaucratic structure. There is little need and less desire to work together. Most bureaucratic systems move institutionally only when they have to, and educational bureaucracies are no exception to this rule. A system of forced collaboration, which these contracts would bring about, can only be to the benefit of the consumer and eventually to the bureaucracy itself. Gallagher has said that such a forced collaboration would immediately affect 4 or 5 percent of the present school population, or roughly half of the population that is perceived as being mentally or emotionally handicapped.

Not only would such a contracting system bring parents into the process of education as never before but professionals could be held accountable for specific goals. Instead of special education being perceived as a place of exile, where problems can be dumped into a wholly separate track, children, parents, and regular educators will perceive it as a special effort, limited to a finite period of time, to help the child meet the schooling ahead.

Gallagher pondered some of the objections to his proposal. The question might be asked, "Why don't parents have responsibilities as well as teachers?" He answers that one function of the contract would be to make explicit the responsibilities of all of the parties involved. Parents and children have responsibilities as well as teachers, and the format of the contract can help to set up specific objectives and goals for parents. Professionals would be acting in a way appropriate to their roles if they helped the parents clarify their own thinking and informed the parents of the child's prognosis so that the parents' goals and objectives were realistic. Professionals would also have to spell out the procedures they would use in getting the child and the system to reach their goals. Collaboration in education can be fruitful. The child's schooling can be strengthened by collaborative efforts, rather than having the respective parties downgrade the efforts of others.

A maximum length of two years in the special-education track has been suggested because there is no evidence that benefits will accrue to the child after this length of time. (It has been discovered that long-term treatment in child psychotherapy leads to emotional attachments that are hard to break. The issue should be whether the child is getting maximum help from the treatment, not whether the employment or emotional needs of the therapist are being met.) Special-education services could still be provided to the child after the end of this two-year period, but the major responsibility for the child's program should revert to general education.

Concern will undoubtedly be raised about what happens if the contract is not honored. There are now few rewards available to school personnel who do their job well, and fewer sanctions for those educators who are not competent, especially those with tenure, and, as fewer new teachers are being hired, there are proportionately more teachers with tenure. The majority of teachers' unions would probably resist the idea of anyone specifying what had to be done or of having anyone judge a teacher's work, but it should also be noted that many teachers would welcome concrete proof of their accomplishments. One of the most debilitating aspects of teaching is the lack of feedback as to effectiveness. Most teachers also recognize that they cannot improve their skills without supervision and instruction.

If the schools did not live up to their contractual obligation, a voucher could be provided to the parent for the cost of the services. Parents would be free to find someone who could do the job and they would not have to pay double tuition—one for taxes and the other for help. If a large body of parents was awarded punitive monetary damages and the school had to pay out large sums of money over its budget for outside services, superintendents and principals would become more concerned with the quality of education that transpires in the classrooms.

Gallagher has stated that his ideas need to be refined—they have been suggested explicitly for special education; there is no reason why they could not be refined and adapted for regular education as well. Establishing concrete objectives would lead to more efficient teaching practices. Accountability is usually thought of in negative terms, as a veiled threat to administrators and teachers, but accountability can include the use of positive rewards for people who do a good job. Vouchers could go to teachers as well as parents. Suggestions of this sort are usually greeted with "Why should we pay someone extra to do what he is supposed to do?" The trouble is that few schools spell out what a teacher is specifically supposed to accomplish, and there is little motivation to perform extra well. Most industries have recognized that it is good business to make things worthwhile for people. Providing teachers with motivation to excel can only help children.

SPECIAL EDUCATORS AS
RESOURCE PERSONNEL

Another approach to working with classroom problems is that of the consulting teacher developed under the leadership of Dr. Hugh McKenzie at the University of Vermont. The approach was designed as part of a special-education program to keep children perceived as moderately handicapped in regular classrooms, rather than having to shunt them off to special classes. The approach could be used for many kinds of educational problems, not just special education.

The University of Vermont trains consulting teachers to use the techniques and principles of applied behavior analysis to measure and monitor children's daily progress in academic subjects and social behavior. The consulting teachers are also trained in curriculum. They learn how to write behavioral objectives that become the minimum performance level for each child. The consulting teachers receive special training in how to train other teachers—on the job—in these same skills, and the consulting teachers are also expected to be able to train parents, aides, students, and school support staff in these same procedures.

The consulting teacher is assigned to a school and he or she is responsible for working with a selected number of teachers within that school. In addition to the direct training that takes place in in-service courses, the consulting teacher is also available for consultation. More than that, this teacher is expected to work directly with children so that effective procedures can be demonstrated, not just talked about. The consulting teacher is not supposed to be an "expert" who is far removed from the child; he or she has to be a competent *teacher*, although his or her primary role is to train regular teachers to solve the problems that they face on a day-to-day basis.

A positive feature of this program is that regular teachers keep the responsibility for working with their "difficult" children. Traditionally, a regular teacher's major task is to identify the exceptional child, and then refer him (sometimes it is a her, but not often) for testing and possible placement in a self-contained special class with a given label such as "mentally retarded," "learning disabled," "emotionally disturbed," and so forth. The regular teacher is then absolved of all responsibility for the child's education. In the Vermont program the students remain in the regular class and are not labeled with any kind of medical terminology. The children do receive help, however, and this is within the framework of general education. Special resources are made available to the teacher and the child, which is considerably better than pretending a problem does not exist. This kind of help can be given to many children—those who are especially creative, especially interested in manual work, and so forth.

Consulting teachers are hired directly by local school districts. Once hired, they can also be a part of the University of Vermont staff, and the consulting teachers are qualified to give graduate courses, for credit, to teachers in the school districts. Courses can be offered at hours that are convenient for school personnel, and the content of some of the courses can be taken directly from the experiences and needs of the teacher. Grades can be directly based on the actual effectiveness of the teachers in their work with pupils.

Classroom teachers usually—and with good reason—act with dismay when a "helper" such as a school psychologist or social worker shows up, because the teachers have learned that "helping" usually means that the teachers will work harder trying to implement a program designed for an individual within the framework of a class of thirty and the "helper" has had little if any experience in working with children. With the consulting teacher, the classroom teacher works with an experienced and well-trained teacher who has put himself on the line and does some teaching of pupils himself, and the classroom teacher can also get training that is relevent, as well as course credit.

Not many universities offer the major part of their coursework directly in education, although most universities claim they teach education courses. If the Vermont model was adopted by other universities, there would be far fewer complaints about "Mickey Mouse" and the dullness and irrelevance of education courses. Local school boards are in a good position to know their own needs, and they must collaborate with universities and state departments of education to change the ossified regulations governing teacher training.

One of the great strengths of the Vermont program is the cooperation which exists between the Vermont State Department of Education, the University of Vermont, and the participating school districts. The university provides special certification for consulting teachers. The state department provides the major portion of the consulting teacher's salary and the salary of aides, thus providing an incentive to hire consulting teachers. The money is more than made up by eliminating many special classes. Vermont is the first state to offer financial incentives for *keeping* children in regular classes, and districts are discouraged from trying to establish and maintain self-contained special classes. The use of financial incentives to keep children *out* of special classes is a far cry from offering personnel and districts financial support for finding deviants. Without a vested interest in deviancy there are likely to be many fewer problems "discovered."

By and large, school districts receive their special-education budgets based upon the number of children that are labeled into educational categories. Virtually all special-education funding is contingent upon a system of educational labels. The more you label, the more you are paid. School psychologists, special education staffs, and many counselors are totally dependent upon this system of labeling, categorizing, and segregating students. Without it they would be unemployed. It is ironic that people ostensibly hired to aid the handicapped are dependent upon discovering and labeling children as handicapped for their very livelihood.

A prime example of paying school districts for producing poor results can be seen in the guidelines for federal funding for educationally disadvantaged schools. The guidelines state that a school is considered disadvantaged if a certain percentage of the students in the school are below grade level in reading. This program will then provide extra funds to that school to develop a reading program to bring the children up to their expected achievement level. As soon as the children reach their expected level the federal funds are cut off for that school. The school's reward for effective teaching is a cutoff in funds that made the increase in learning possible. The only means of continued access to these federal funds is to have a reading program that keeps children below their anticipated achievement level.

The federal government and the various states should pay districts for the results they achieve. School districts should receive a bonus for reducing the number of deviants in the schools. If a district can integrate emotionally disturbed students back into regular classrooms and teach them to achieve, the district should receive a financial bonus for solving the problem. If districts received incentives for reducing deviancy rather than producing it, children would be served better. Districts unable to reduce deviancy or improve reading scores would be penalized financially for their poor results.

HELPING PARENTS SELECT
SPECIAL-EDUCATION PROGRAMS

More and more children will probably be enrolled in special-education programs as state legislatures and courts mandate that school districts must provide education for *all* children, including the severely physically and mentally handicapped. But not all schools will provide quality education for handicapped children. Some parents have found themselves in the position of having to move to a different school district to ensure an adequate education for their children.

Mr. and Mrs. Charles Michael had three children. The middle child, Michelle, was severely handicapped. She had been diagnosed as brain-injured, moderately cerebral-palsied, hyperactive, and retarded. Michelle was eight years old and was able to recognize only a few letters and colors. She could not add or subtract and could count only by rote.

Mr. Michael worked for the Texas Rangers and moved frequently. The quality of Michelle's schooling varied tremendously. At one time Mr. Michael was stationed in a small border town and the children in the school district tormented Michelle unmercifully. Even some teachers treated her with contempt, and she was finally placed on home instruction. The Michaels decided to move from that town, but they also decided that they would move only to a school district with a good special-education program.

Mr. Michael explained the situation of Michelle's schooling to his supervisor and requested a transfer. There was an opening in Wheeling, Texas, a town of 15,000, and his supervisor said that Mr. Michael could transfer there if he wanted to.

The Michaels decided to take three days off and visit the school system. They called and made an appointment with the director of special education for the Wheeling Cooperative School District. The director told the parents that they had programs for children like Michelle and they had dealt successfully with many children like her. This was extremely encouraging to the Michaels, since many school districts had thrown up their hands in horror at the mention of a handicapped child.

Mr. and Mrs. Michael were quite impressed with the special-education director. He had a long and successful background in special education, including five years of teaching, a principalship, and finally promotion to the directorship. He explained how each program for handicapped youth operated in the district and how they tried to meet the needs of each child. Obviously a great deal of thought had gone into the planning for each program. Wheeling had formed a cooperative unit with four other districts, and they ran programs for many kinds of handicaps, including deaf-blind, multihandicapped, and severely mentally retarded. It was easy for the Michaels to see that the director was quite proud of his program and he was eager for them to visit the class that Michelle would be in. The director himself took the Michaels to visit the class. Michelle was to be placed in a class for multihandicapped youth, with a maximum of eight students in the classroom. The class had a full-time teacher and a full-time teacher aide. The Michaels were very pleased with the teacher's understanding of and empathy with their problem. They also observed children quite similar to Michelle and felt that she would be able to adjust to the class.

The classroom appeared to be well organized, and the children had appropriate learning tasks on their own level. Some of the children were learning to tie shoes, others were learning self-care skills, and one or two were beginning academic programs. Every child had a sequentially programmed speech-development course.

From past experience Mrs. Michael knew that one test of a district's special-education program was the feelings of the parents who had children in the program. She asked the director of special education if he could provide her with the names of two or three parents who had children in the class. She said she would like to discuss with them how they felt about the class and the services provided by the district. The director was a bit surprised by her request, but gave her the names of three parents with children in the same class that Michelle would attend.

Mrs. Michael called the parents in the afternoon and arranged to meet one of the mothers personally. All three of the parents were extremely pleased with the educational program and the services provided by the district. One of the parents even commented that he had had the opportunity for a promotion in his job but had turned it down, since he would have had to move his child away from his current school placement.

The Michaels eventually moved to Wheeling and they, too, were extremely pleased with the placement. Their experience shows that parents can develop screening techniques—albeit crude ones—to determine the effectiveness of special-education programs. These techniques can be used before parents move to a new area; they can also be used by parents to evaluate the effectiveness of a program that their children are attending.

Depending upon the severity of the child's handicap, there are several guidelines that parents can follow in evaluating a special-education program. If it is a program for moderately handicapped youth, one of the first things the parents should look at is the achievement test scores. Parents can get this information from teachers, the school principal, or the director of special education. Most districts use some method of achievement testing, and while they will not divulge individual scores, they should be able to show the *average* gains in reading, math, and spelling. Most programs dealing with the moderately retarded, learning-disabled, or emotionally disturbed should be able to get at least a six months' gain in reading for a full year in the program. A good program should be able to get more than that. If the program average is less than six months' growth in one year, it is questionable if this program will be able to help a child in academic areas such as reading, spelling, or math.

Parents should also visit the director of special education. Mr. Michael commented that before he moved to another district he would want to talk to the head man; he felt that if the head man was competent and enthusiastic about the program, then probably the program would be good. If the director appeared to be incompetent or had doubts about any program he was responsible for, it would be highly unlikely that it would be a good one.

Parents can also visit school principals to try to determine their effectiveness in dealing with handicapped youths. Many principals will admit that they do not like to work with the handicapped and only reluctantly have them in their schools. This will mean that there is little likelihood of integration with regular-class students. A reluctant principal may also mean that there would be a lack of support for the teacher or the class. If the parents find this kind of attitude on the part of a principal, they should visit the director of special education and express their concern.

Parents can also visit the class that their child will be attending. If the child is already attending a special-education program, the parents should make at least three or four visits during the school year for a minimum of thirty minutes each visit. In addition to the visits, the parents should have a conference with the teacher in the middle of October to determine how the child is adjusting to the new school year. A second conference in January to evaluate progress and a concluding conference in May or June to determine the child's future school placement are also helpful. Parents can also encourage teachers to contact them if there are any problems or a specific area where the parents might be of assistance.

Most districts have admissions and discharge committee meetings on all children. Many states allow parents to attend these meetings if they wish to do so, and attendance can be very helpful. At the meetings, parents will hear the actual reports on their child's school progress and the reasons for placement in a current program. Parents can more adequately assess the appropriateness of current placement if they are aware of the professional's perception of their children. Parents may add pertinent information that the committee is unaware of. Permission to attend these meetings can usually be achieved through the school principal.

If a parent is unhappy with a program or placement, he may request to have his own psychologist or lawyer attend the admissions and discharge committee meeting. California and several other states now require school districts to allow such professionals to attend the meetings.

Many states now give a stipend to parents of handicapped children if their school districts do not provide special-education programs. There has consequently been a dramatic increase in the number of private schools in this area. Some of these schools are excellent. Others are simply bad.

It would be wise for a parent who is considering enrolling his child in a private school to inquire whether the school is accredited and by whom, and to use the more informal criteria that the Michaels used in their evaluation of Michelle's school. Some specific steps for parents to take and criteria to keep in mind are:

1. Visit and talk with the director of the school to assess his skills, abilities, and interest in dealing with the handicapped. Parents should be well aware of the educational background

of the director and his experience as a teacher and administrator of programs for handicapped youth. Many of the new private schools are hiring retired military personnel and public school personnel who have had no actual experience in teaching or working with the handicapped.

2. The parents should get a complete list of staff members who are going to work directly with the children. Again, the parents should know the background, experience, and education of all staff members. Generally speaking, it would be beneficial if staff members were experienced in working with exceptional youth.

3. Parents should visit the classroom to assess the quality of the facilities. They should be especially aware of whether adaptations have been made for the physical or mental handicaps of the children. Parents should visit a number of the classes in the school, and on different occasions.

4. Parents should get a list of at least four parents who have sent children to the school. It would be wise to telephone some parents and meet others. If there is a parent group, it would also be beneficial to go to one of its sessions.

5. Parents can also discreetly inquire of local community agencies and professionals about their perception of the school.

A NEW ROLE FOR MENTAL HEALTH SPECIALISTS

Mental health workers are generally employed by school systems to work with deviant pupils. The bulk of their work consists of testing, working on committees to facilitate special-class placement, writing reports, traveling from school to school and meeting to meeting, counseling and psychotherapy, and leading groups such as sensitivity or encounter groups.

Extremely large portions of budgets are spent on their activities, even though they "benefit" only a few people. Taxpayers can no longer afford to subsidize a system where so many children fail within that system. We are compelled to pay for programs that have not worked in the past and will very likely not work in the future. In order to save children and money, it would be better to make mental health workers more effective in the schools, and to give them new roles to play.

Most school psychologists, social workers, and guidance counselors would probably even welcome a change in their roles. The futility of administering test batteries to pupils for referral to nonexistent resources must be recognized by testors as well as the testees and their teachers. The recommendations resulting from many psychological testing sessions are so general that they are not particularly helpful to teachers or pupils, and many people would welcome the opportunity to do more than be a part of the labeling process or administer psychotherapy to children who do not welcome or need that kind of help.

School psychologists and their allied professions can contribute to effective education if they are willing to shed their expert-dummy roles—the psychologists being the experts and their patients the dummies—and become more responsive to the needs of the schools they are supposed to serve. This cannot be done if clinicians continue to work on an itinerant basis, showing up at a school once every few weeks or so, and spending the majority of their time working with individual pupils. Clinicians can only be effective if they look at the system in which the child operates.

Psychologists have frequently noted that when a child in one classroom is referred for special-class placement, merely transferring him to a classroom across the hall can alleviate the problem. The teacher's behavior and perception of the child's behavior can have a profound effect in the classroom. To diagnose and effect changes in teaching situations that create failure, clinicians need to become experts in classroom procedures, behavior modification, and curriculum so that the environment can be changed, and a system created that fosters growth toward specific goals.

One concrete way that school psychologists, guidance counselors, and the like can do this is by helping teachers, children, and parents to clarify their goals and establish a mutual expectancy of what they want out of the schooling process. This is not an easy task, but when goals are complementary they are much easier to reach than when they are different. Differences should be negotiated, not resolved through power. A great deal of vituperation and hurt feelings usually accompany school disputes, and often a third party can be instrumental in the resolution of these disputes. When all of the parties involved in school transactions learn to focus on specific objectives, schooling can be more productive for all concerned.

Teachers are often in a good position to know how to use mental health personnel, but custom prevents anyone other than administrators from prescribing the job of the mental health personnel. If these administrators would let different kinds of services evolve, the role that psychologists play might be more productive.

In the Visalia Unified School District in California, the director of Guidance and Psychological Services, Gerald Jolley, has instituted a no-referral system of psychological services. In a no-referral system, the school psychologist comes to the school on a regularly scheduled basis. The staff determines how to use the psychologist's time. They can choose to use the psychologist for testing individual children. But teachers quickly realized that it was to their benefit to have the psychologist play a wider and more vital role.

At most schools they formed a guidance committee to do the preliminary screening of children formerly done by the psychologist. This guidance committee tries to solve the problem *before* the case is referred for outside services. The guidance committee can change the child's classes, drop classes, provide suggestions to the classroom teacher, or request that the teacher or counselor have a conference with the parents so they might work together on any problems in the school. The guidance committee has been able to solve more than 80 percent of the problems that have been referred to it and that in the past would have gone directly to the psychologist. The cases not solved by the guidance committee are referred to the school psychologist, who still works with the committee. The psychologist is used as a resource to the guidance committee.

The use of the guidance committee and the no-referral system quickly changes the role of the psychologist from that of testor to that of school-wide consultant. The psychologist is present during teachers' meetings. He is also present during lunch hour and can observe children on the playground and during physical education. The psychologist is able to identify practices detrimental to the development of children. For example, one youngster was having difficulties in reading, and the school psychologist, after two or three teaching sessions with the child, was able to institute a specific phonics program and a token economy for the youngster. The psychologist was able to implement a change from a basal reading program to *Distar Ready* (a Groves phonics program published by SRA). Psychologists have been able to take data on the amount of work accomplished using different seating arrangements, and they have been able to make concrete recommendations on how the furniture should be situated so children would not bother each other and the teacher whenever they needed to get materials or have their work checked.

Under this procedure, the psychologist is more cognizant of the needs of the teaching staff and is made more responsible to the teacher, since he is on the school site at regular intervals and will be there to hear about it if his work and suggestions are not valid. The frequent comment "Yes, but what do you do when the school psychologist leaves?" is no longer appropriate, because the psychologist will be coming back. The ongoing consultant role where the psychologist works directly with the teacher requires the psychologist to be exacting in this work, since he will be around to see its results. The case study loses its importance as teachers become more skillful in working with the child who is perceived as deviant.

Teachers also have different attitudes toward those psychologists who work directly with staff and those who work primarily with students, without any teacher direction. A survey taken in 1972 showed that teachers much preferred to work with the psychologists who worked with them. The staff that worked directly with the psychologists found: (1) they were helpful personally; (2) they provided services of a practical nature; and (3) the teachers were more inclined to work with the psychologists. The staff that were in situations where the psychologists worked directly with the children found the psychologists: (1) not very helpful with concrete problems and (2) not very competent; and (3) the staff were also not very confident about the ability of the psychologists to do very much for the children.

A primary benefit of having the psychologist work on an ongoing consultant basis is that he receives feedback about the effectiveness of his performance. He must meet the needs of the school, or they have the option of deciding not to use him at all. Here is a case where at least some of the consumers of educational services have a direct voice in the kind of product they receive, and it has worked to the benefit of the teachers, the children, and even the psychologists themselves.

There will undoubtedly be times when diagnostic work is necessary for individual pupils, but this work must be done by those who are responsible for implementing the programs. It is too easy to make mistakes in diagnoses and end up with labels and with reports that have little meaning for actual practice. But if the diagnostician had to take responsibility for putting his or her ideas into practice, we would see less glibness in reports and more concrete suggestions that would be feasible to implement.

Education is striving to become a science, but as of now there are many gaps in our knowledge and too many variables over which we have little or no control. Because of this, we will have to do a great deal of tinkering. It might be necessary to place children in special programs, but this can be done on a trial basis instead of on a semi-permanent basis. The psychologist can also be made responsible for evaluating the effects of a particular program on a child. If that program does not work, then it is incumbent upon the school to make the appropriate changes.

Psychologists are in a particularly good position to evaluate program effects. A good deal of the training they receive is in the area of measurement and research. Rather than their being used as clinicians, they could probably be more effectively used in the area of evaluation. They could help school people set out objectives and make sure that these objectives are measurable. They can then use existing instrumentation or devise methods to measure the rate of progress toward these goals, the cost-effectiveness of the approach, and whether any unwanted side effects were accruing because of the approach.

PSYCHOLOGISTS AS ECOLOGISTS

Mental health personnel can also play a positive role in educating the public at large and teachers in particular about "mental illness" and social deviancy. For years mental health specialists have proselytized that mental health is an illness that strikes one out of ten people. Psychiatrists and psychologists have pursued the medical conception of illness with a rare kind of vigor and have frightened people into believing that mental illness is a disease that may afflict anyone. Many naïve people even believe that the "disease" is contagious.

While the clinicians' intentions were undoubtedly good, it is unfortunate that they succeeded so well. Despite their pleas and admonishments to the general public to be tolerant of "sick" people, virtually every study in the area has documented that the public does not trust or want anything to do with people who have been perceived as "mentally ill." Those who have undergone psychiatric or psychological treatment in a public institution have been subject to a loss of prestige and often jobs, and there have been serious curtailments of their civil rights and civil liberties. This treatment has also been extended to schoolchildren. Many teachers and administrators react with horror and dismay, and often with punitive attitudes and behaviors, to those children who have undergone any kind of public and sometimes even private treatment. They want these children to be taught by clinical workers and segregated from other, "normal" children.

School clinicians can now take the opposite tack and alert the public and teachers that "mental illness" deals with the goodness of fit between the perception of behavior and the behavior itself, not with pathology. They can instruct people that the perception of the behavior cannot be divorced from the behavior. They can explain to teachers how mores change, and that what was considered as pathology is now accepted as differences in lifestyle. Pathology need not be invoked at all to understand or explain or treat most behavior.

Dr. Bill Rhodes of the University of Michigan has suggested that the education of the "emotionally disturbed" child should be geared not only to the stressor, but also to the strained members of the culture, so that the agitated exchange between culture violator and culture bearer that we now call pathology can be interrupted. He has suggested that mental health workers enter into the living units in which the child functions, whether that living unit be the classroom, family, or neighborhood. The mental health worker could act as a buffer, and through demonstration and interpretation, he could also be a model of how to interact with the "disturbed" child. The clinician can both help the child change behaviors that trigger off emotional reactions on the part of others and help others to be more tolerant of differences, and more accepting of diversity. The following is a direct example of this.

Cindy bounced into her seventh-grade science class. She beamed when she saw that some of her friends were already waiting in the room.

"Hi. Hey, what do you think we are going to do today? Are you going to the football game after school? I like that dress."

Cindy continued to chatter, not waiting for an answer to her first question before she asked two more. It was obvious that the other girls liked Cindy even though she was a nonstop talker with her peers.

The girls continued their talk until the teacher came into the room. As he called out the names on the roll, Cindy hissed at the boy sitting next to her, "Hey, Charlie, do you still love Julie?"

Charlie blushed noticeably as the other students around him giggled.

"All right, knot head," the teacher called out to Cindy. "Just knock it off for the rest of the day or out you go."

Cindy put her head down for a moment as the teacher continued to call the roll. The teacher was almost through calling out the students' names when a "psst" interrupted him. He looked over his glasses at Cindy. "Now look, knot head, I already told you once to shut up. Now get out of here and sit under the table."

"But, Mr. Winton," Cindy pleaded, "I'll be quiet. Honest I will. I won't say anything else, honest I won't."

"Out! Out!" the angry teacher replied.

Cindy walked out of the room as some class members smiled and others hung their heads in fear of being next.

After class was over, Mr. Winton went to the office and talked to Allen Hall, Cindy's counselor. "Look, Allen," Mr. Winton said. "If you don't do something about Cindy Wilson I'm going to flunk her in my third-period science class."

Allen looked surprised and told Mr. Winton that Cindy was one of the most talented students in the school and in the district's program for mentally gifted minors.

"I don't care what she's in, that girl's a pain. She never shuts up from the moment she puts her foot in the door."

"Okay, Mr. Winton. I'll talk to her this afternoon to see what I can do."

Allen called Cindy in during sixth period. "Hi, Mr. Hall, how are you?" Cindy bubbled, as she came into the office.

"I have to talk to you about your class with Mr. Winton, Cindy."

"Oh, that class. Isn't there some way you can get me

out of there? No one likes that class. He's always calling us knot head or stupid or some other name like that. None of the kids like that class."

"Look, Cindy, I can't change you now, and you know it. I think I'll come into class for a while tomorrow and observe."

After visiting the class, Allen did determine that the teacher was very negative with the students and frequently called them names. He also saw that Cindy talked out in class an average of eighteen times per fifty-five-minute period.

Allen Hall had his first conference with the teacher. "I see what the problem is with Cindy, Mr. Winton. She talked out an average of eighteen times on every one of my visits. I'm going to have a conference with her this afternoon."

"That's good. I hope you can do something with her. That girl is about to drive me nuts in that class."

"There's another problem in your class, Mr. Winton."

"Oh? What's that?"

"You are very critical of the students. You made thirty-five negative comments on the average, and only five positive comments. You also call them names like stupid, knot head, dummy, and ignorant. I think if you tried to be more positive with the kids and compliment them when they do what you want, you would be able to see the behavior that you would like to see."

Allen Hall had four more conferences with Cindy and two more with the teacher. He got the teacher to understand that Cindy was a very gifted young girl and also very enthusiastic. She did her work accurately, neatly, and correctly. She was always one of the first ones through with her work. As soon as she finished, she started talking to the other students in the class.

Mr. Winton started using Cindy as a tutor for the other students when she finished her work. She was able to talk and use her ability in a constructive way. Mr. Hall also worked with Cindy and had her count the numbers of times she talked out in class. Mr. Hall was able to reduce Cindy's talking out and she was made the class monitor. Cindy ended up with an A in the course and was sent out of the room only two more times during the entire semester. Mr. Hall also worked with the teacher on methods of increasing his positive comments to the students.

The clinician can work to change the schools as well as to change the child. But the clinician, as well as all of the people involved in school transactions, should be accountable for their behaviors and they must be required to *demonstrate* that they have changed the behaviors and the perceptions of people. That is, the psychologists themselves will have to look at the whole system in which a child operates, and then specify what measurable objectives they are striving toward, and how effective they have been in their work. In any kind of systems analysis it is imperative that no one be placed in a superordinate position, ostensibly outside of the system.

With that perspective in mind, clinicians can also engage in administrative work and set up programs within the school. They can set up learning centers and arrange course credits for youngsters who want to study things on their own or apprentice themselves to practitioners—be they artists, psychologists, mechanics, carpenters, or what have you. The clinician can help coordinate these activities and establish behavioral objectives that the learner will have to master. These programs will eliminate much of the social deviancy and academic failures that transpire in schools now.

Clinicians can help discover the abilities that students

possess and help the students shift their roles from that of learner to teacher. Many children in schools have a great number of skills ranging from how to tie macramé knots to electronics or higher mathematics. These children should be allowed to teach courses within the school for credit. The youngsters who teach these courses should themselves receive credit for teaching—if they can demonstrate that their students did master the skills that were taught.

Psychologists can also work toward a reform of the grading system, which does so much to create psychological and social problems. Rather than consigning a certain number of children each year to failure and disesteemed statuses, psychologists can work toward testing programs for academic subjects that allow each child to master the subject matter and receive an A for his or her effort. If the goal of the school is to have students master material, then the rate at which they pick up these skills becomes secondary. Those students who do not do well on tests should have the opportunity to restudy the material and take the tests again and again until they have learned the material. Many teachers need help in writing good tests, and psychologists can be quite helpful in this aspect of schooling. This means that the school will no longer be preoccupied with ranking children, but will be more concerned with the actual teaching process.

Psychologists can also work with vocational and prevocational placement. Up to now vocational education has been thought of as a dead end for children and was usually reserved for those students who did not do well in school. But even the most academically talented children can learn a great deal from practicing artisans and professionals, and the psychologist can help to match up those who want to learn and those who want to teach.

7

Punishment and Motivation for the Exceptional Child

A Gallup poll taken in the latter part of 1972 has indicated that discipline is a major concern for educators, and that parents consider the lack of discipline to be a primary weakness in our educational system. Nearly 50 percent of parents and teachers queried felt that children have *too many rights*.

Discipline, however, is often taken to mean the necessity of punishment. Any person punished has two basic modes of response, somewhat simplistically labeled as *fight or flight*. Flight is usually physically manifested when children run away from home in fear of a beating, or are truant from school in order to avoid physical or verbal punishment from either peers or teachers. But a more frequent method of flight is into the world of fantasy, an escape route that most of us use at one time or another. Finding the world of fantasy much more comforting and satisfying than the intellectual world in which they actually live, many children spend a large portion of their time "lost" in fantasy. Unfortunately daydreaming is punishable, and so the time spent in that world exposes them to the possibility of the same forms of disciplining that made them prefer it in the first place.

Fighting can also be manifested directly in the form of a physical attack on the child's "captors"; a less obvious attack might be witnessed in purposeful academic failure. Children, like most of us, feel that such behavior punishes those who have punished them.

We have let ourselves become accustomed to the eruptive violence of children since it is so pervasive. Some children have been *taught* to hate teachers or police, whites or blacks, males or females, or sometimes *everyone* indiscriminately. This is to say that angers are cyclical; angry children strike out, and when their victims retaliate, there is more cause for anger, and the process is repeated. In the use of punishment to maintain discipline, then, any teacher must be careful to see that the punishment is not simply another form of anger.

In children, anger is thrust not only at institutions but toward adults in general. Wanton assaults, arson, burglary, and muggings pervade suburban as well as urban areas. Sections of large cities are terrorized by roving bands of adolescents who molest and assault victims. Other children turn their anger inward. Drug abuse, which can be a self-destructive act, has increased to the point where drug overdoses have become one of the leading causes of death in the teen-age group, and children as young as eight are known heroin addicts.

The anger and despair of children are displayed in many ways, and in the schools they are often made manifest by vandalism. Schools must budget millions of dollars for vandalism, enough money in some systems to pay the salaries of scores of remedial-reading teachers. Building schools without windows has become commonplace, not for aesthetic reasons, but because the anticipated cost of broken glass dictated architectural style. Attendance officers in some schools are overwhelmed by their case-loads, and truancy has become a life-style for children as young as eight or nine, many of them becoming chronic truants who simply never attend school.

The significance of these facts lies in the continuing cycle. Parents or teachers who abuse children were often themselves abused as children; children who do poorly in school are often repeating the patterns of their own parents or teachers. The anger felt by victimized children will vent itself later in some other fashion. Our schools, which represent a basic socializing force, must interrupt this cycle by creating discipline without anger.

Punishment can be effective as a short-term solution to suppressing behavior, but motivation is usually more effective in building behavior. Motivating students can be a key factor in teaching them appropriate social and academic behavior. Teachers and parents will often say that a child who is not meeting their expectations "doesn't care" or that he has "a bad attitude." Such statements are usually born out of frustration and are an indirect admission of teacher and/or parent failure. Furthermore, motivation is assumed to be a basic character trait that cannot easily be changed, and the "defect" is seen to be a characteristic of the child rather than residing in the situation.

If motivation is defined as the degree of willingness to engage in particular behaviors, then it definitely can be changed. The easiest way to change motivation is through the use of contingencies. The principles upon which these changes can be brought about were best summarized by an experimental psychologist, Dr. David Premack. The Premack principle is that "any response A will accelerate any response B if and only if the independent rate of A is greater than that of B, and if the high-probability behavior A is made contingent on the low-probability behavior B." In essence, this means that acts of high probability such as eating candy will reinforce acts of low probability such as washing hands, but only if the candy is made contingent upon first washing hands. This principle is the same that teachers and parents have used intuitively throughout history, and it is why wise parents will allow their children to watch television only *after* they have completed their homework.

When Premack's principle is used systematically, it has resulted in substantial improvements in social and academic behavior on the part of children that were considered exceptional. This has been accomplished both in the home and in the school, and sometimes by having the home and school work together. In schools the Premack principle is put to work by making high-probability behavior such as recess, gym periods, games, and monitor jobs contingent upon the acceleration of low-probability behavior such as learning long and short vowels, reading, and learning two-place division. In the home, parents can make high-probability behavior—that is, behavior that the child will probably engage in, such as play, going on a trip to the zoo, watching television, and so forth—contingent upon the child's successfully learning all the number facts that the teacher has assigned, or writing a composition.

In one school program, a child began to encounter difficulty with mathematics and started to harbor an intense dislike toward the subject. He rejected all suggestions of help from his teacher and every day told his teacher that he would study the subject at home and be prepared for tomorrow's lesson. The teacher decided not to push this matter, as the child had had a good work record in previous years and was an able student.

After three weeks, however, when the child did not do any of his assignments, the teacher decided that Johnny was losing out on important skills that were prerequisites for additional skills, and this lack of competency would only solidify his dislike of mathematics.

The teacher requested a parent conference and the parents and teacher decided to set up a home-school cooperative contingency program to help Johnny through this difficulty. The teacher was quite explicit in her assignments to Johnny and each day sent a note home to the mother detailing whether he had correctly completed his assignment or not. There were twenty-three schooldays before Christmas vacation and the parents and teacher decided that Johnny had to complete successfully sixteen lessons if he was to go on a ski trip with his parents. If he did not complete his assignments, he would go with his parents on the vacation, but he would not be allowed to ski.

The teacher first made sure that the mother was able and willing to use this contingency and would follow through on her verbal statements. When the mother said she was willing to do this, the teacher then advised her *not* to nag Johnny to complete his assignments or even ask if he had finished them. Instead, the mother and teacher made quite clear to Johnny the consequences of his behavior and also let him know quite clearly that they were both willing and able to help him.

For the first few days of the program Johnny did almost no math and kept on complaining that he couldn't understand any of it. At the same time he did not want any specific help. His mother and teacher merely repeated that they were ready to help him with any *specific* problem. Johnny soon realized that they were serious about the contingency and began to work on his math. He found that there were many parts of his assignment that he could do, and many things that he could not do. He began to ask for help on those specific problems and ended up completing nineteen of his assignments.

At the same time he found his work getting easier and easier as he understood more and more. He soon regained his former academic prowess and even began to ask for extra assignments.

Teachers will often contact parents when there is a problem, but it is easier to solve the problem when a specific program and contingencies are employed, and this is far more effective than merely decrying the failure.

A daily report card can serve several functions. It gives the student a concrete and immediate record of his performance and it serves to stimulate feedback from the teacher. The daily report gives the parents a concrete indication of the child's performance and can help to structure the interaction between the parents and the child, particularly if the contingencies have been made explicit beforehand. Parents can be trained to couple social reinforcement with material reinforcement, so that eventually a more "natural" kind of reinforcement can take place.

Not all parents are as cooperative and effective as was Johnny's mother. One study found that approximately 25 percent of the parents worked with in a training program had too many problems of their own to carry through a contingency program effectively. In many homes the parents do not control effective reinforcers for their children. This becomes more and more true as children get older and they begin to rely on the peer group for support and counsel. In such an event, the school can operate programs for children where the entire peer group can be worked with directly. The peer group can help to shape the behavior of its members in a more appropriate manner. Such a project has already been accomplished by Dr. John Burchard of the University of Vermont. Burchard and his colleagues worked with junior high school youngsters who were having difficulty adapting to the school and/or the community. Difficulty in adapting was defined as having had contact with the police for antisocial behavior and/or receiving less than a C average or having more than twenty-five absences during the school year.

A "youth center" was set up during the evening hours in a junior high school and membership was restricted to only those children who received invitations from their friends to join the club. The initial membership was composed only of children who had had difficulties in the same junior high school. The center was staffed with college undergraduate students, who received credit for their work in the center. During the first part of the evening, the youth center offered arts and crafts, library activities, gym events, and other recreational activities. During the latter half of the evening, the lounge was changed into a coffeehouse. Candles were set up, and music for dancing was provided. In addition, a snack bar was set up where children could purchase snacks. A token economy was used within this setup, and it was found that this procedure was quite effective in managing the behavior of the children. Of especial significance in this project was the fact that attendance was all voluntary and no form of coercion was used. Once this was accomplished, Burchard and his colleagues began to extend the earning of points into the school itself so that increased attendance, higher grades, and more appropriate deportment resulted in more tokens for the youngsters and more opportunities to participate in the youth center.

The results of this last project are not in yet, but they appear to be quite encouraging. This seems like a fruitful approach for schools to try, for special education, as it is practiced today for the moderately handicapped, appears to be very much on the wane, and the schools must begin to recognize this.

PUNISHMENT WITHOUT VICTIMS

Any animal, if punished severely enough, will strike out at the nearest object. This reaction has no bearing on whether the new victim is responsible for the punishment. In a similar way, children will attack the "system" by singling out an innocent person.

Any form of child abuse is questioned here, not only because of its savagery but because such forms of punishment have been proven empirically ineffective. What they accomplish is to give the victimized child a model of violence for dealing with problems, and that model is then replayed to fellow students, teachers, and eventually to the child's children. Certainly there are times when punishment procedures are called for, but never when they are to be used as a cathartic release of frustration.

Many children come to schools filled with hatreds and violence that must be handled by teachers immediately, with little recourse to theory or idealistic pronouncements. A teacher faced with a pupil who is beating up smaller children, or extorting money, or defacing school property, has no choice but to take some form of immediate action.

Punishment is effective only when the person punished understands the relation between his behavior and the punishment that follows. It should therefore be meted out with immediacy and consistency. Research indicates that it is often ineffective to accompany a reprimand with expressions of rage and disgust. Above all, punishment must not be used to convince children that they have to be "bad" in order to deserve adult attention.

One of the ways to avoid the trap of having punishment increase unwanted behaviors is to take data regarding the effectiveness of the punishment. This is to say that the term "punishment" includes not only evaluative but also empirical elements. For instance, behaviorist psychology treats punishment as a response, which, if delivered contingently with a particular behavior, will decrease the probability of the recurrence of that behavior; but, to avoid a circular argument, behaviorists also state that the punishment procedures should be able to reduce the occurrence of other classes of behavior as well. From an empirical point of view, a teacher's humiliation of a child by means of punishment cannot be known to reduce the undesirable behavior without a background of data showing the direction of the change.

Some psychologists have found that when reprimands are sharply and publicly delivered to students, the amount of disruptive behavior actually increases, but that softly and privately delivered remonstrances do succeed in decreasing obstreperous behavior. Another study found that when a teacher doubled the use of punishing phrases, instances of misbehavior tripled.

Safeguards against the use of punishment might include the following: review committees to consider any suggestion that punitive measures be used in any specific case; justification by teachers and/or administrators as to why particular behaviors should be discouraged; and, perhaps most importantly of all, a provision that the child's side of the picture be given unbiased representation so that the full context of all of the behaviors can be more readily understood and changed.

The more a program is structured to reinforce children for positive behavior, the less need will be found for punishment. But teachers should know how to use punishment so that, if it has to be used, unwanted side effects are not generated. Positive reinforcement of behavior that is incompatible with the behavior that the teacher wants to punish is unlikely to result in a response of either fight or flight, and the undesirable behavior in question will decrease as well.

THE POWER OF EXCLUSION

One rather arbitrary practice that schools use against exceptional children is to expel or suspend them. The Supreme Court noted in the *Green* vs. *Gal* case that the suspension of a student—just one step short of expulsion—"brings to bear the terrible organized forces of the state, just as surely as it is applied by the police, the courts, the prison warden, and the militia." In regard to suspensions, the concept of due process is practically foreign to our educational establishment. Many systems do not even provide hearing procedures in actions that culminate in suspensions. Principals of schools are allowed to suspend children for as long as five days without having to justify their actions, and many principals suspend the same student repeatedly—which amounts to a *de facto* expulsion in the absence of any requirements for hearings. Theoretically at least, appeals are possible, but before they are held, the punishment has already been administered. But according to a Supreme Court ruling, students are entitled to notice, an opportunity to be heard, and a chance to defend themselves against specific charges in the face of injurious government acts. The burden of proof, however, is placed on the child, whose parents, in most cases, are the least likely to be able to afford legal advice.

When *The New York Times* analyzed more than one

hundred cases of school suspensions in 1971, it found none in which the school board's recommendations had been totally observed. The *Times*'s editorial on the subject (February 20, 1971) states:

> *The study by the New York Civil Liberties Union of 115 instances in which pupils were suspended last year from their schools, adds up to a serious indictment of the system's disciplinary practices. Students' rights in many cases appear to have been given short shrift. The fact that in one year 14,000 suspensions took place raises questions why this form of punishment was so exclusively used.*
>
> *Causes for suspension .... ranged from the ridiculous to the outrageous. To suspend a student for irregular attendance seems like prescribing liquor for an alcoholic. . . . City educators, who are rightly alarmed by a growing trend of students' lawlessness and contempt for authority, should be particularly alert to the damage done to respect for law and justice by official example.*

The Center for Law and Education at Harvard University has suggested a list of procedures to protect the child perceived as deviant that could be followed in suspension hearings. The Harvard Center recommends:

1. A written statement of charges that will be presented to the student and his parents.
2. A hearing before the individual charged with the misconduct where the student will be allowed to inspect any documents and evidence. The student, his parents, and his representative should be allowed to inspect any documents used at the hearing.
3. Students should be allowed to hear the evidence against them and to question those witnesses that are accusing them.
4. The student should be able to use counsel if he wishes, and the counsel should be able to cross-examine witnesses fully.

The counsel should be able to present a defense for the student.

5. The schools should appoint a hearing officer to determine the guilt or innocence of the student, and should put their findings in writing.

Suspensions and expulsions are always accompanied by official entries in "the record." School officials frequently use the pupil's record to coerce, threaten, and dampen criticism of the system. While records can assess pupil progress and learning deficiencies, they can also be used to damage a student's success in school, his college acceptance, or his job placement. Official records are often hidden from parents and pupils, but are sometimes completely open to others.

Anecdotal records of students, which are usually irrelevant to academic progress, are frequently misused—especially by minimally trained guidance counselors, who normally compile them. In too many cases, biased information—such as that provided by prejudiced teachers—is included in the reports as fact. Typically, anecdotal records include material reciting major instances of misconduct—for example, talking in class, chewing gum, or refusing to salute the flag. Parents have found the following in their children's files: "a bed wetter"; "his father is a black militant"; and "a real sickie—abs. truant, stubborn and very dull . . . is verbal only about outside irrelevant facts. . . . Can barely read. . . . Have fun." Such records—or such expectations—remain with a child from the age of six onward.

The American Civil Liberties Union asserts that parents have the right to inspect records and not merely have items from records read to them by school officials. Parents have the right to challenge the accuracy of school data about their children. In many states, students' confidential records may not be given to a third party without written parental consent. Schools should be judicious in the preparation of the school records, especially those regarding a child's personal or family life. Negative statements should not be included in the student's records that follow him from school to school, and it is best to separate academic records from disciplinary files. Rather than recording negative findings, systematic and direct observation of a child's behavior is a more effective means of helping the school and the child combat deviant behavior.

If parents are concerned about school records, they should contact the local school principal and follow the administrative hierarchy up the ladder to the superintendent and the school board. If they are still barred from viewing their child's records, the parents should seek legal assistance from their own attorney or from the American Civil Liberties Union.

OBSERVATION

One of the most crucial roles that mental health workers can play is that of an objective observer in school systems. Much of what transpires in schools would be changed immediately if people were aware of what was going on. People get locked into self-defeating patterns of behavior, but they are not conscious of what they are doing to contribute to these patterns and do not have the objectivity to see what they are doing that is nonproductive or harmful. The context of behavior is not examined thoroughly. For example, when supervisors rate or work with teachers, it is primarily the teacher's behavior that is examined. But teaching is not an isolated phenomenon, it is an interaction *between* people, and the behavior of the individual cannot be fully understood without an examination of that interaction.

An instrument to study this interaction was developed by Dr. Ian Spence. This instrument enables an observer to note teacher behavior in reaction to pupil behavior. An adaptation of this instrument is shown in Figure 2.

Using this instrument, tally marks are made by the observer as the specific teacher and pupil actions that are being monitored are emitted. Spence's interaction matrix has the advantage of identifying patterns of behavior, and it does not put the onus on only one party. It is relatively easy, or at least easier, to devise intervention programs from the data available in the matrix, since a great deal more knowledge is available than if the child or the teacher alone were observed. Teachers can know how to change their own behaviors if they are responding in an unsuccessful way to the child's behavior. The same skills can be taught to the child if he or she is aware of how his or her behavior is exacerbating a situation instead of ameliorating it.

The observer merely records the teacher or pupil behavior in the cell that denotes the teacher or pupil reaction. Frequencies of the behaviors can then be tabulated to give a picture of what each party is contributing to a situation. The effects of an intervention program can be ascertained by continuing to take this data after the program is put into effect. The data can then be compared to the child's or the teacher's baseline performance—or with any other reference group with which they want to make comparisons.

For example, in a second-grade class, Mrs. R. had a particularly difficult time with Tyrone. He would frequently shout out answers, giggle, and talk to his neighbors so loudly that it became annoying to other chil-

PUPIL-TEACHER INTERACTION COMPLIANCE PINPOINTS

Teacher: A: _____ B: _____

Observer: _____

Date of Obs: _____

Time Stop: _____

Start: _____

Total Time: _____

Direct Obs: ◯ T.V. ◯

PUPIL ACTIVITY

dren. To counteract this, Mrs. R. would often sit Tyrone next to her during group work and had him sit right next to her desk when the class was doing individual assignments or working together as a whole.

This procedure was not effective, however, and when Mrs. R.'s aide took data on the interactions between Mrs. R. and Tyrone, it was discovered that inadvertently Mrs. R. placed her hand on Tyrone's shoulder every time he began to talk out. Conversely, she seldom paid any attention to him when he was working.

They hypothesized that the physical contact Tyrone received served as a reinforcer for his loud and obstreperous behavior, and that her ignoring of his working behavior served to decrease the length of time that he did work.

Mrs. R. decided to reverse this, and she ignored his loud talk and giggling and placed her hand on his shoulder when he was working. The procedure proved to be quite effective and Mrs. R. felt that the data she received from her aide was instrumental in changing her behavior and consequently Tyrone's.

Aides, teachers, and children can also be trained to use this instrument. Using this instrument as a model, adaptation for specific situations can be constructed and objective data sought. The teacher and his or her pupils can fill in what behaviors need to be observed. The rest consists of adequately training the observers. There is no correlation between years spent in school and the capability of observing.

Many school systems have paraprofessionals working in the classroom, but the teachers do not know how to make good use of their assistants. Training paraprofessionals in specific observation skills can be an important approach to upgrading the quality of education in classrooms.

The approach of using specific observations is also helpful to teachers and children, and at the same time it avoids labels. It is quite different to talk about a child who fought twelve times in an hour or left his seat fourteen times during a math period than it is to talk about a child with minimal brain damage or paranoid schizophrenia. Knowledge of the latter labels will not be helpful to a teacher in terms of shifting his or her own strategies or behaviors, but concrete knowledge of what the teacher did after a pupil behavior was emitted, and a graph showing the rate of acceleration or deceleration of the specific behavior in question, can be extremely helpful because they are so objective.

There are no panaceas in education today, but some methods work better with some teachers than others. Some teachers can use methods that would be disastrous if used by other teachers. Teaching styles are quite idiosyncratic, as is learning style. But we can document how teachers behave in a class, and then attempt to find *better* ways of doing things if we are not satisfied with the results of the *status quo.*

Sound measurement systems are scarce in educational practices. This applies to cost effectiveness data, interactions between teachers and pupils, how well school systems meet their stated goals, the effectiveness of personnel who receive taxpayers' money, and how much and what children learn.

A measurement technology does exist, however, and we need to put it into use. The combination of allowing children and parents and teachers choices about their education and then using a yardstick to measure what we are getting can qualitatively improve the schooling of American children and, consequently, the quality of life in our society. The rights of children would also be better protected under such a system.

8

"How Much Did You *Learn* Today?"

We are in a time when some of the most fundamental premises of public education have begun to come under attack: the single curriculum, for instance, the heritage of all Americans, which constitutes the mark of an "educated" man. Educators are beginning to question the wisdom of *forcing* adolescents to attend school where they are compelled to study a curriculum that is meaningless to them. Millions of children in the United States spend tens of millions of hours memorizing theorems for geometry, which they promptly forget after the test is over. The lists of useless information seem endless, but what students now want to learn—and cannot because of time pressures—also seems endless.

Even the school's most vociferous supporters in the past, the college-educated and affluent, have joined the

ethnic minorities' and taxpayers' revolts with a revolt of
their own: they no longer support increased budgets and
new bond issues. At the same time, their children are
prominent among those who question the value of a formal education.

The schools are in deep trouble as the usual sources
of their support dry up. They have antagonized minority
populations in many urban centers. Certain schools have
actually become armed camps in a war between the establishment—symbolized by school administrators, re-
mote boards of education, and teachers' unions—and students and militant parents. While violence and the
turning of schools into armed camps are not the way the
problem is manifested in the suburbs, another form of
revolt occurs there as children smoke marijuana between
classes in the bathrooms, and swallow "uppers" and "down-
ers" between Cokes in the school cafeteria.

A noted scholar, Dr. Carl Bereiter, claims that
schools are experiencing more and more difficulty because of two factors. The first is a sophisticated detach-
ment within our society that makes it impossible for the
rituals of schooling to be honored. As schooling, with its
regimentation, recitals, rules, and hierarchies, appears
more and more absurd and archaic from the outside, the
inside is also affected, and isolated little worlds with their
own arbitrary rules (such as monasteries, secret societies,
and so forth) collapse and die. The second important factor is the 20 to 30 percent of students who actually dislike
and even hate school. We are living in an age when dis-
satisfied minorities will no longer be docile and listen to
the boss. Behavior modification, if used well, will enable
this group to get what they want out of school, and at the
same time educators will be able to teach these children.

Another reason for the current difficulties of the
public schools is their failure to teach basic skills. Bereiter

takes the British infant schools and the open-classroom concept to task, because, while they have alleviated some of the coercion and ritualization in schooling, they have not advanced new solutions for teaching skills. The advocates of the open-classroom approach contend they do as well as traditional schools in teaching basic skills. However, some 10 to 20 percent of the school population suffers from skill retardation, and better approaches are needed to help this group. Once again, behavior-modification methods can be instrumental in ensuring that this group learns skills and masters the tools of learning.

Bereiter claims that skills have not been taught simply because schools have devoted themselves to the education of "the whole child." When the schools concern themselves with training, they are quite successful—namely in athletic teams, bands, and driver education. There skills are stressed, and it is a rare student who does not improve his skills in any of these areas. The goal of training, which can be defined as the ability to perform specific tasks, gets lost in the rituals of schooling and in assignments with little relation to the school's training goals. We need to do more than use the space in the corridors if we are to qualitatively improve life and training in schools—and eliminate much of the deviancy for children in our society.

One way of cutting down on the amount of deviancy in the schools is through specially devised instructional materials that take into account the individual needs of the learner. The United States Office of Education has recently helped in the formation of Special Education Instructional Resource Centers. These centers harbor thousands of pieces of curriculum materials—many of which have been field-tested—which can accommodate the individual learner. Introducing such materials in the classroom can cut down on the need to practice whole-group instruction, which is so devastating to many children who need to follow a curriculum at their own pace.

Another way of cutting down on some of the deviant behavior within the school is to increase the options for each child within the school. As of now, schools can be compared to the bed of Procrustes. Either the child fits the program or he is stretched or shrunk. It would be more feasible to stretch the kinds of programs available so that the learner can study many things, in many ways, and curriculum and programs could be molded to fit the individual. The setting of behavioral objectives for *each* child would allow the individual to flourish, something we have talked about for decades but seldom followed in practice. Even special education can offer a variety of plans to meet the needs of the individual child. Right now special-education programs are usually of the either/or variety. Either the child is placed in special classes or he is left to flounder in the educational mainstream.

Dr. Evelyn Deno has proposed a cascade system that would allow a number of options for the exceptional child, ranging from almost complete integration to hospital or homebound instruction. Her plan includes the following options:

> Enrollment in regular day classes with special-education instructional materials and, if necessary, special consultative services to the regular teacher.
>
> Enrollment in regular day classes with itinerant teachers working with the child, or placement in a special-resource room for selected periods during the school day.
>
> Enrollment in a special day class or a special day school.
>
> Enrollment in a residential school, or homebound or hospital instruction provided.

Pupils would move up the ladder as rapidly as possible and would move down the ladder as slowly as possible. All placements would be on a trial basis, and the school must demonstrate that the child is moving toward concrete goals; if the school cannot demonstrate that the child is making progress, they must place the child in an alternate program. Behavior modification, with its emphasis on clearly stating the objectives of programs, can be quite helpful in providing criteria and evaluation methods for these trial placements.

Those professionals who are responsible for a child's treatment must also take the responsibility for his placement and diagnosis, and the schools must recognize that the use of etiological labels, borrowed from other disciplines such as psychiatry and medicine, to establish homogeneity, have no place in the school.

Every child is unique and every child deserves special education. To think that identical IQ scores or medical labels make children homogeneous is simply erroneous. We must relate to children on the basis of their educational needs, not on the basis of their disability labels. Even the use of pre-tests and diagnostic tests to ascertain just what it is that students have to learn would ensure greater objectivity and less stereotyping in teaching.

As mentioned repeatedly throughout this book, behavior modification is not a panacea for all of our educational ills; but it is a methodology that can go a long way toward improving some of the difficulties the schools now encounter. Schools can become more effective now if teachers, administrators, and school-board members could receive training in the methodology of behavior analysis. The systematic use of reward and punishment and an emphasis on measuring progress could eliminate much of the fumbling that now accompanies the educational process. This training could also be applied to the support staff of schools, such as attendance officers, social workers, and business managers.

Curriculum reforms could be instituted in classes for

the nonhandicapped as well as for the handicapped. In many areas there is such great pupil mobility that the majority of the pupils enrolled in school at the end of the academic year were not enrolled in the same school at the beginning of the year. If the same sets of texts were used throughout school systems, pupils would be able to learn more efficiently and teachers would not have to waste hours trying to place children in materials that they will not use for very long. Comprehensive curriculum planning needs to be done throughout systems—not just in single classes and grades.

Incentives also need to be developed to encourage teachers and administrators to devise new organizational structures that will enhance learning and minimize deviant behavior. Evaluation specialists need to be a part of this planning. Incentives can be given to researchers to collaborate with school districts in the drafting and implementation of such plans.

Most important of all, we need to recognize that educational reforms and strategies, delivered noncontingently, will *not* overcome the inertia and vested interests that make up all bureaucracies. Only coordinated efforts, with systematic use of rewards and punishments, will effect major reforms. Reinforcers—whether they are in the form of money, free time, recognition, or what have you—need to be applied to schools as well as to children, and *performance,* not rhetoric, needs to be focused upon.

The big mistake that education makes—and this includes regular education as well as special education—is to concentrate on inputs. That is, there is too great a concern on what goes into education—teacher certification, number of hours of instruction, what the course of study should be, and so forth. What we need to look at much more closely is output. What happens to the children in the school? How well have they mastered skills? How many have failed to learn socialization skills? How many children are considered deviant? If contingencies could be applied to outputs with as much force as they are applied to inputs, education would become much more effective.

We have become overly concerned with the quantity of education programs and have neglected quality. Those programs which cannot demonstrate their worth should simply be abandoned and replaced with some of the programs described in this book. Such programs, which allow individualization of instruction, could do a great deal to eliminate the problems of the exceptional child.

The research literature is quite clear that children who receive positive reinforcement do better. The same things can be applied to schools, and we should reinforce the good things that schools do.

A VIEW TOWARD FREEDOM AND UNDERSTANDING

What do we expect schools to accomplish? What should be the purposes of education? It is easy to describe the function and operation of existing schools, and even easier to criticize them for their practices—especially for what they fail to do. The objective of this book, however, is to be constructive and to set out alternatives to our present system of education so that practices might be improved. Behavior-analysis methods provide the most feasible alternatives to current education programs.

Currently schools place great emphasis on conforming behavior. The rules in schools are legion, ranging from how to head a paper to receiving bathroom passes. Even in academic work great emphasis is placed on conforming behavior. One interesting study found that teachers would ask open-ended questions but would punish students if their answers were offbeat or showed evidence of divergent thinking. Only answers that could be placed in a yes/no framework were acceptable.

In an ideal school, greater emphasis would be placed on innovation. Teaching conformity leads to student rigidity—an inability to adapt to new methods of learning. It would seem that man's greatest ability is his adaptiveness. Those societies which could not adapt to changing climatic or social conditions or new discoveries and inventions—the Eskimo or Pygmy societies, for example—remain static and exist only marginally.

With the technological revolution still in process and traditional structures like family, school, and work changing beyond recognition within a matter of decades, man needs to adapt to changing surroundings more rapidly than ever before. Instead of schools emphasizing conformity to rules and regulations with little adaptive value—styles of dress, waiting in line, doing "busy" work, or satisfying no-think requirements—schools should reinforce and reward creative activities and the discovery of new ways for solving problems.

Education should be a liberating process. It should free children not only from ignorance but from feelings of inferiority. Education should teach that what we *know* is minute compared to what we *can know,* and that we need not accept what we *don't know* as being *unknowable.* Education should help people make decisions consonant with their own feelings and interests. It should teach people to order their own social structure so that there is neither blind obedience nor blind hatred of authority. Childhood is not only preparation for adult life; it is a significant part of life in its entirety. A person in school is not only a learner preparing for the future, he is a person living in the present a very vital portion of his total life span. Childhood deserves to be a happy and fulfilled time in everyone's life, and schools should construct the conditions that allow for maximum growth and fun in learning.

The amount of time spent in the schoolhouse could change radically. Children might leave school at an earlier age, and teen-agers and adults should have the option open for returning to school at different times during the course of their lives. School could also show as great an interest in avocation as in vocation.

One of the first questions asked about educational innovations is how much they cost. There is no reason why the programs described here need cost any more than does our current system—there is even the possibility that costs would be reduced.

Reduction in the amount of schooling required is inherent in many systems described in this book and proves one immediate solution to the problem of funding. In addition, the money currently spent on education could be used to help more people than it does: it costs an average of $1,500 per year to send a child to school in suburban areas, and close to $10,000 per year to keep a child in a correctional institution.

If we multiply $1,500 times 13, which for our purposes could be considered the length of stay per years in public schools for each child, it would cost $19,500 for the state to provide education for each child. However, there is some evidence that children could learn nearly as much in half the amount of time presently spent in school. (In a study in Norway, an experimental group spent only half time in school as the control group. Achievement differences between the two groups were minimal, scarcely worth the doubled costs, not to mention the boredom for the control group.) If schooling could be cut in half, or to any great extent, for each child—and this is probably a conservative estimate—enormous amounts of money already channeled into schools would be released for a different, more benevolent, and certainly more efficient kind of education.

A DIFFERENT KIND OF SCHOOLING

We now recognize that a major function of schools is to provide custodial care for children while adults work. Given the current form of our economy, this means we must provide day care for children. The plan to cut schooling does not mean that children would have to be left unattended. While further achievement in reading, for instance, does not seem to be enhanced by further schooling, children could learn different skills and study a wider array of subject matter. Instruction in computer technology, art, electronics, and other branches of knowledge could still be accomplished. Recreational programs and avocational subjects could be upgraded and treated as more than a frill. Children could also learn through doing by our recognizing that education does not have to be confined to what transpires within the school's walls. Apprenticeships could be worked out with local businesses, skilled workers, and professionals, and children could pick up valuable skills and course credit through such programs; in this way their time would be productively and safely spent.

A different kind of schooling is also important if we recognize that our economic structure is in the process of rapid change, and that attitudes will eventually have to keep up with these changes. There will be less need for "work" as automation becomes the norm. Automation itself would occur more rapidly and more effectively if there were not such widespread opposition to its successful application. If workers were given new kinds of employment, such as going to school, there would be less reluctance to see the distasteful and repetitious aspects of work mechanized.

Unemployment in our changing economy is *not* limited to those who are undereducated or illiterate. Education or lack of education is not the fundamental deterrent to job fulfillment for everyone. The spectacularly high unemployment rates of the late 1960s and early 1970s show that Ph.D.'s comprised a large part of the unemployed, and highly educated people in particular industries, such as aerospace, found themselves without meaningful work. College professors in fields such as history or foreign languages were equally hard pressed.

If certain attitudinal shifts could be made, there would be less need for work as we know it. Education can play a major role in helping us shift our thinking from the belief that everyone must work and that only the lazy, the shiftless, the neurotic, and the uneducated fail to find gainful and meaningful employment on a full-time basis. Man must learn how to live with leisure, and the schools can help avoid the new type of anomie that might accompany such a change. Reallocation of resources and different kinds of programs could make the schools more functional.

Both the implicit and explicit objectives of the school system can be changed. Schools should be less concerned with conferring prestige and social privilege, and more concerned with the mastering of avocational and vocational skills. The needs of the learner should be paramount. At the same time, the business of education needs a broader community base. The educational guilds would still have an important part to play, but they would be judged by how well they accomplished their mission. People would be free to learn through routes alternative to the school system. If the objectives of schooling were made clearer, greater emphasis could be placed on mastering the objectives, and less emphasis placed on conforming to school rituals.

Some people learn better from reading, some from listening, some from seeing, some from doing. Reading is certainly an important skill and schools should rightly pursue their quest to teach every child how to read. Given the University of Kansas Follow Through model and other programs, schools already know how to do this. But we should at the same time recognize that reading is diminishing in importance as television and other media fulfill a person's need for recreation and information, and a great deal of instruction can be given through media other than books. Literacy requirements in societies change. We need to keep abreast of what constitutes literacy in *today's* society, not yesterday's.

Given the fantastic array of educational technology available, it should be possible for each individual to learn in his or her own style. A certain portion of the schools could operate in part very much as libraries and clubs—such as a French club in a high school or college, a voluntary organization where people gather to increase their knowledge and skills. Like libraries, schools could operate so that both the locale and the materials for education would be available on weekends and in evenings as well as during the day. If a child wants to learn about rocks, the librarian does not stipulate, "You must come here every morning between ten and eleven o'clock, and only during that hour can you learn about rocks." Similarly, the librarian does not say, "You must read this book first," or "We will have a test every Thursday." In the library the child decides for himself what he wants to learn, how he wants to learn it, which books are too difficult for him, which books are not appealing to him. Disciplinary problems in the library are also minimal. The child does not leave the library with a feeling of shame or inadequacy.

When the schools accept that they have to work *with* people and not *on* them, education will become less of a battleground and more of a collaborative effort. When it is recognized that the learner is a key ingredient in the schools and will be respected for his efforts, education will become an eagerly sought activity. When an ecological approach to social deviancy is accepted, the number of aberrant behavers will diminish.

A system of checks and balances needs to be introduced into the schools, the same system that has proved remarkably effective in our government. At one time, administrators had too much power in our schools. Teachers had too little. At present, administrators and teachers are working to keep power only for themselves. The consumer must share that power. The necessity for reform is urgent, yet without some kind of power base all the consumer can do now is say, "Please."

One way that consumers can exert power is through the budget. Consumers can insist that schools get paid only for what they deliver. Accountability in meeting objectives will go a long way toward making school officials do a better job. The voucher system will give the consumer an important voice in how the schools are run. Parents and children do not support summer camps that offer bad programs. Why should they continue to support inadequate schools?

Businesses that want to continue operating cannot afford to ignore technology. Schools will also have to utilize our natural and technological resources if they want to stay in business. They will no longer be able to use technology to promote docility and conformity. When people pay directly for products, they will not ask their children, "Did you *behave* today?" The question will become, "How much did you *learn* today?" And that is what schooling is all about.

Notes

1 Children Who Need Help

P. 2. For example, *see* V. Hall, D. Lund, and D. Jackson, "Effects of Teacher Attention on Study Behavior," *Journal of Applied Behavior Analysis, 1,* 1 (1968): 1–12.

P. 3. Dr. Montrose M. Wolf of the University of Kansas was the consulting psychologist. Joy Graubard was the teacher.

P. 6. For a good discussion of behavior modification, *see* L. Ullmann and L. Krasner, *Case Studies in Behavior Modification* (New York: Holt, 1965), especially the introduction.

P. 7. K. D. O'Leary and R. Drabman, "Token Reinforcement in the Classroom: A Review," *Psychology Bulletin, 75,* 6 (1971).

P. 7. D. Baer, M. Wolf, and T. Risley, "Some Current Dimensions of Applied Behavioral Analysis," *Journal of Applied Behavior Analysis,* I (1968): 91–97. *See also* E. Hanley, "Review of Research Involving Applied Behavior Analysis in the Classroom," *Review of Educational Research, 40,* 5 (1970): 597–626.

P. 9. Dr. Donald Bushell, Jr. Lecture given at a graduate symposium in behavior analysis, Department of Special Education, Yeshiva University, New York, 1973.

P. 11. R. Benedict, "Anthropology and the Abnormal," *Journal of General Psychology, 10* (1934): 59–82.

P. 13. *See* R. Rosenthal, and L. Jacobson, *Pygmalion in the Classroom: Teacher Expectation and Pupils' Intellectual Development* (New York: Holt, 1968). There are substantial methodological problems in this work, but their general findings appear to be true. *See also* W. V. Beez, "Influence of Biased Psychological Reports on Teacher Behavior and Pupil Progress" (Unpublished doctoral dissertation, Indiana University, 1968), for a substantiation of Rosenthal's hypothesis.

P. 14. R. Edgerton, *The Cloak of Competence* (Berkeley: University of California Press, 1967).

P. 14. J. Mercer, *Labeling the Mentally Retarded* (Los Angeles: University of California Press, 1972).

P. 16. E. H. Auerswald, "The Interdisciplinary vs. the Systems Approach in the Field of Mental Health." Paper presented at the American Psychiatric Association, 1966.

P. 23. J. Rabkin, and R. Rabkin, "Delinquency and the Lateral Boundary of the Family," in Graubard, P. (ed.), *Children against Schools* (Chicago: Follett, 1969).

P. 23. J. L. Johnson, "Special Education in the Inner City: A Change for the Future or Another Means for Cooling the Mark Off?" *Journal of Special Education,* 3 (1969): 245.

P. 24. W. W. Lewis, "Continuity and Intervention in Emotional Disturbance: A Review," *Exceptional Children, 31,* 9 (1965): 465–476.

P. 24. The research which discusses the efficacy of special class placement for the "moderately retarded" is summarized by Lloyd Dunn in "Children with Mild General Learning Disabilities" in L. Dunn (ed.), *Exceptional Children in the Schools,* 2nd ed. (New York: Holt, 1973). *See also* R. L. Jones, "Labels and Stigma in Special Education," *Exceptional Children 38* (March 1972): 553–564.

P. 24. These figures are taken from an article by Iver Peterson, "Columbia Dedicates a Building to Help Teach Handicapped." *The New York Times,* November 25, 1973, 66.

P. 26. *See* R. Barker and P. Gump, *Big School, Small School* (Stanford: Stanford University Press, 1964).

2 Children Can Change Schools

Pp. 29–30. *See* P. Graubard, H. Rosenberg, and M. B. Miller, "Ecological Approaches to Social Deviancy" in B. Hopkins and E. Ramp (eds.), *A New Direction for Education: Behavior Analysis* (Lawrence, Kansas: Department of Human Development, 1971). *Also see* F. Gray, P. Graubard, and H. Rosenberg, "Little Brother Is Changing You" in *Psychology Today, 7,* 10 (March 1974): 42–46.

P. 49. *See* T. Brigham, "Notes on Autonomous Environments: Student Selected vs. Teacher Selected Rewards" (Unpublished paper, Department of Psychology, Washington State University, Pullman, Washington). *Also see* J. Felixbrod and K. D. O'Leary, "Effects of Reinforcement on

Children's Academic Behavior as a Function of Self-Determined and Externally Imposed Contingencies," *Journal of Applied Behavior Analysis, 6,* 2 (1973): 241–250.

3 Behavioral Approaches at Work

P. 55. S. Alson, "A Curriculum for Teaching Elementary School Students the Scientific Method of Inductive Reasoning for Personal Management" (Unpublished Masters Project, Department of Special Education, Yeshiva University, New York, 1972).

P. 55. *See* T. Brigham, P. Graubard, and A. Stan, "Analysis of the Effects of Sequential Reinforcement Contingencies in Aspects of Composition," *Journal of Applied Behavior Analysis, 3* and *4* (1972): 421–430.

P. 58. *See* D. Bushell, *Behavior Analysis Teaching* (Englewood Cliffs, New Jersey: Prentice-Hall, 1973).

P. 61. See A. Givner and P. Graubard, *A Handbook of Behavior Modification for the Classroom* (New York: Holt, 1974), especially Chapter 5.

P. 62. D. Bushell, "The Right to Choose," A Behavior Analysis Background Paper (Follow Through Project, Lawrence, Kansas: University of Kansas).

P. 68. The research on this aspect of the program was compiled by B. Geer (principal) and J. Kovaly (Follow Through coordinator), C. S. 6, Bronx, New York.

4 Teaching Adaptive Behavior

P. 81. *See* T. Brigham, "Notes on Autonomous Environments: Student Selected vs. Teacher Selected Rewards" (Unpublished paper, Department of Psychology, Washington State University, Pullman, Washington).

P. 82. Personal communication given on a snowy afternoon by Charles Salzberg and Sally Rule in the Kansas City airport, January 1971.

P. 82. J. Kozol, "Free Schools: A Time for Candor," *Saturday Review,* March 4, 1972, 51–55.

P. 90. S. Minuchin, P. Chamberlain, and P. Graubard, "A Project to Teach Learning Skills to Disturbed Delinquent Children," *American Journal of Orthopsychiatry, 37* (1967): 558–567.

P. 98. M. A. Lewis, R. E. Kifer, D. R. Green, J. B. Roosa, and E. L. Phillips, "The SOCS Model: A Technique for Training *Achievement Place* Students in Complex Communication Skills" (Paper presented at American Psychological Association, Montreal, Canada, 1973).

P. 101. *See* P. Graubard, "Utilizing the Group in Teaching Disturbed Delinquents to Learn," *Exceptional Children, 36* (1969): 267–272. *Also see* P. Graubard, P. Lanier, H. Weigest and M. B. Miller, "An Investigation Into the Use of Indigenous Grouping as the Reinforcing Agent in Teaching Maladjusted Boys to Read," Project No. 8-0174, 1971. Final report to the United States Office of Education.

P. 102.   *See,* for example, H. W. Polsky, *Cottage Six* (New York: Russell Sage Foundation, 1962).

Pp. 102–103.   Aimee Graubard, "Changing Parent Behavior" (Paper submitted to Special Education seminar, Yeshiva University, Spring 1972).

P. 104.   For a more extended discussion of this topic, *see* A. Givner and P. Graubard, *A Handbook of Behavior Modification for the Classroom* (New York: Holt, 1974).

5 Programs That Can Make a Difference

P. 108.   J. F. Glasser, *The Elementary School Learning Center for Independent Study* (West Nyack, New York: Parker Publishing Company, 1968).

P. 117.   W. Georgides, "Individualized Instruction," *Thrust,* Association of California School Administrators, *2,* 5 (April 1973).

P. 117.   *See* G. Poirier, *Students as Partners and Team Learning* (Berkeley: Center of Team Learning, 1970.)

P. 121.   R. M. Whitehead, "How the Young Are Taught in China," *Saturday Review,* March 4, 1972, 17.

P. 125.   W. Glasser, *Schools without Failure.* (New York: Harper & Row, 1969.)

P. 128.   E. Jenkins, "A School Voucher Experiment Rates an 'A' in Coast District," *The New York Times Magazine,* May 29, 1973, 70.

P. 130.   A. Graubard, "The Free School Movement." *Harvard Educational Review, 42,* 3 (August 1972).

P. 131.   J. Kozol, "Free Schools: A Time for Candor," *Saturday Review,* March 4, 1972, 51–55.

6 Special Education Can Be Special

P. 137.   J. Gallagher, "The Special Education Contract for Mildly Handicapped Children," *Exceptional Children, 38,* 7 (1972): 527–536.

P. 137.   F. M. Hewett, *The Emotionally Disturbed Child in the Classroom* (Boston: Allyn & Bacon, 1968).

P. 137.   F. M. Hewett, "Teaching Speech to an Autistic Child through Operant Conditioning," *American Journal of Orthopsychiatry, 35,* 5 (October 1965): 927–936.

Pp. 137–138.   N. Hobbs, "Helping Disturbed Children: Psychological and Ecological Strategies," in H. Dupont (ed.), *Educating Emotionally Disturbed Children* (New York: Holt, 1969).

P. 138.   J. Gallagher, "The Special Education Contract for Mildly Handicapped Children," *Exceptional Children, 38,* 7 (1972): 527–536.

P. 142.   L. Christie, H. McKenzie, and C. Burdett, "The Consulting Teacher Approach to Special Education: Inservice Training for Regular Classroom Teachers," *Focus on Exceptional Children, 4,* 5 (October 1972): 1–4. (Denver, Colorado: Love Publishing Company).

P. 156.   T. Wither, "Attitudes of Teachers towards Psychological Services as

Measured by Osgood's Semantic Differential" (Unpublished doctoral dissertation, University of Southern California, 1968).

P. 159.   W. C. Rhodes, "The Disturbing Child: A Problem of Ecological Management," *Exceptional Children, 33* (1967): 449–455.

P. 159.   W. C. Rhodes, "A Community Participation Analysis of Emotional Disturbance," *Exceptional Children, 36* (1970): 309–316.

7 Punishment and Motivation for the Exceptional Child

P. 164.   F. Hechinger, "Discipline Is Again the Main Concern," education section, *The New York Times,* September 3, 1972.

P. 167.   D. Premack, "Toward Empirical Behavior Laws: I-Positive Reinforcement," *Psychology Review, 66* (1959): 219–233.

P. 169.   G. R. Patterson, J. A. Cobb and R. S. Ray, "A Social Engineering Technique for Retraining the Families of Aggressive Boys," in H. Adams and L. Unikel (eds.), *Georgia Symposium in Experimental Clinical Psychology,* Vol. II (Springfield, Illinois: Thomas, 1972).

P. 170.   J. Burchard, P. Harig, R. Miller and J. Amour, "New Strategies in Community-Based Intervention" (Paper delivered at Symposium on Behavior Modification, National University of Mexico, Mexico, January, 1973). To appear in E. Riber (ed.), *The Experimental Analysis of Delinquency and Social Aggression* (New York: Academic Press, in press).

P. 172.   K. D. O'Leary and W. Becker, "The Effects of the Intensity of a Teacher's Reprimands on Children's Behavior," *Journal of Social Psychology, 7* (1969): 8–11.

P. 172.   D. Thomas, W. Becker and M. Armstrong, "Production and Elimination of Disruptive Classroom Behavior by Systematically Varying Teacher's Behavior," *Journal of Applied Behavior Analysis, 1* (1968): 35–45.

P. 173.   N. Hentoff, "Why Students Want Their Constitutional Rights Now," *Saturday Review,* May 22, 1971, 60–73.

P. 174.   *The New York Times,* February 20, 1971, education section.

P. 174.   Reported in R. Klemer and G. Neal, *Special Report on Education in the United States* (Washington D.C.: National Schools Public Relations Association, 1972).

P. 175.   *Bill of Rights for High School Students* (Maryland: Civil Liberties Union Association, 1968), distributed by Association of High School Counselors and Principals.

P. 177.   I. Spence, "Counting the Teacher Reactions to Pupil Behaviors: A Tool for Teacher Training" (Unpublished doctoral dissertation, Yeshiva University, New York, 1972).

8 "How Much Did You Learn Today?"

P. 182.   C. Bereiter, "Schools without Education. *Harvard Education Review, 42,* 3 (1972): 390–413.

P. 184. E. Deno, "Special Education as Developmental Capital," *Exceptional Children, 37* (1970): 229–237.

P. 189. T. Husen, "Does More Time in School Make a Difference?" *Saturday Review,* April 29, 1972, 32–35.

References

ALSON, S. A. "A Curriculum for Teaching Elementary School Students the Scientific Method of Inductive Reasoning for Personal Management." Unpublished master's project, Department of Special Education, Yeshiva University, New York, 1972.

AUERSWALD, E. H. "The Interdisciplinary vs. the Systems Approach in the Field of Mental Health." Paper presented at the American Psychiatric Association, 1966.

BAER, D., WOLF, M., and RISLEY, T. "Some Current Dimensions of Applied Behavioral Analysis." *Journal of Applied Behavior Analysis,* I (1968): 91–97.

BARKER, R., and GUMP, P. *Big School, Small School.* Stanford: Stanford University Press, 1964.

BEEZ, W. V. "Influence of Biased Psychological Reports on Teacher Behavior and Pupil Progress." Unpublished doctoral dissertation, Indiana University, 1968.

BENEDICT, R. "Anthropology and the Abnormal." *Journal of General Psychology, 10* (1934): 59–82.

BEREITER, C. "Schools without Education." *Harvard Educational Review, 42,* 3 (1972): 390–413.

BRIGHAM, T. "Notes on Autonomous Environments: Student Selected vs. Teacher Selected Rewards." Unpublished paper, Department of Psychology, Washington State University, Pullman, Washington.

BRIGHAM, T., GRAUBARD, P., and STAN, A. "Analysis of the Effects of Sequential Reinforcement Contingencies on Aspects of Composition." *Journal of Applied Behavior Analysis,* 3 and 4 (1972): 421–430.

BURCHARD, J., HARIG, P., MILLER, R., and AMOUR, J. "New Strategies in Community Based Intervention." Paper delivered at Symposium on Behavior Modification, National University of Mexico, Mexico, January 1973. To appear in E. Riber (ed.), *The Experimental Analysis of Delinquency and Social Aggression.* New York: Academic Press.

BUSHELL, D. *Behavior Analysis Teaching.* Englewood Cliffs, New Jersey: Prentice-Hall, 1973.

BUSHELL, D. "Behavior Analysis." Lecture given at graduate symposium, Department of Special Education, Yeshiva University, New York, 1973.

BUSHELL, D. "The Right to Choose," A Behavior Analysis Background Paper. Follow Through Project. Lawrence, Kansas: University of Kansas.

CHRISTIE, L., MC KENZIE, H., and BURDETT, C. "The Consulting Teacher Approach to Special Education: Inservice Training for Regular Classroom Teachers." *Focus on Exceptional Children, 4,* 5 (October 1972): 1–4. Denver, Colorado: Love Publishing Company.

CIVIL LIBERTIES UNION ASSOCIATION. "Bill of Rights for High School Students." Maryland: Civil Liberties Union Association, 1968. Distributed by Association of High School Counselors and Principals.

DENO, E. "Special Education as Developmental Capital." *Exceptional Children, 37* (1970): 229–237.

DUNN, L., ed. *Exceptional Children in the Schools,* 2d ed. New York: Holt, 1973.

EDGERTON, R. *The Cloak of Competence.* Berkeley: University of California Press, 1972.

FELIXBROD, J., and O'LEARY, K.D. "Effects of Reinforcement on Children's Academic Behavior as a Function of Self-Determined and Externally Imposed Contingencies." *Journal of Applied Behavior Analysis, 6,* 2 (1973): 241–250.

GALLAGHER, J. "The Special Education Contract for Mildly Handicapped Children." *Exceptional Children, 38,* 7 (1972): 527–536.

GEORGIDES, W. "Individualized Instruction." *Thrust,* Association of California School Administrators, 2, 5 (April 1973).

GIVNER, A., and GRAUBARD, P. *A Handbook of Behavior Modification for the Classroom.* New York: Holt, 1974.

GLASSER, J. F. *The Elementary School Learning Center for Independent Study.* West Nyack, New York: Parker Publishing Company, 1968.

GLASSER, W. *Schools without Failure.* New York: Harper & Row, 1969.

GRAUBARD. A. "The Free School Movement." *Harvard Educational Review, 42,* 3 (August 1972): 351–373.

GRAUBARD, P., ROSENBERG, H., and .MILLER, M. B. "Ecological Approaches to Social Deviancy." In B. Hopkins and E. Ramp (eds.), *A New Direction for Education: Behavior Analysis.* Lawrence, Kansas: Department of Human Development, 1971: 80–101.

GRAUBARD, P., LANIER, P., WEISERT, H., and MILLER, M. B. "An Investigation into the Use of Indigenous Grouping as the Reinforcing Agent in Teaching Maladjusted Boys to Read." Project No. 8-0174, 1971. Final report to the United States Office of Education.

GRAUBARD, P. "Utilizing the Group in Teaching Disturbed Delinquents to Learn." *Exceptional Children, 36* (1969): 267–272.

GRAY, F., GRAUBARD, P., and ROSENBERG, H. "Little Brother Is Changing You" in *Psychology Today, 7,* 10 (March 1974): 42–46.

HALL, V., LUND, D., and JACKSON, D. "Effects of Teacher Attention on Study Behavior." *Journal of Applied Behavior Analysis, 1,* 1 (1968): 1–12.

HANLEY, E. "Review of Research Involving Applied Behavior Analysis in the Classroom." *Review of Educational Research, 40,* 5 (1970): 597–626.

HECHINGER, F. "Discipline Is Again the Main Concern." Education Section, *The New York Times,* September 3, 1972.

HENTOFF, N. "Why Students Want Their Constitutional Rights Now." *Saturday Review,* May 22, 1971, 60–73.

HEWETT, F. M. *The Emotionally Disturbed Child in the Classroom.* Boston: Allyn & Bacon, 1968.

HEWETT, F. M. "Teaching Speech to an Autistic Child through Operant Conditioning." *American Journal of Orthopsychiatry, 35,* 5 (October 1965): 927–936.

HOBBS, N. "Helping Disturbed Children: Psychological and Ecological Strategies." In H. Dupont (ed.), *Educating Emotionally Disturbed Children.* New York: Holt, 1969.

HUSEN, T. "Does More Time in School Make a Difference?" *Saturday Review,* April 29, 1972, 32–35.

JENCKS, C., et al. *Inequality.* New York: Basic Books, 1972.

JENKINS, E. "A School Voucher Experiment Rates an 'A' in Coast District." *The New York Times Magazine,* May 29, 1973, 70.

JOHNSON, J. L. "Special Education in the Inner City: A Change for the Future or Another Means for Cooling the Mark Off?" *Journal of Special Education*, 3 (1969): 245.

JONES, R. L. "Labels and Stigma in Special Education." *Exceptional Children*, *38* (March 1972): 553–564.

KLEMER, R., and NEAL, G. Special Report on Education in the United States. Washington D.C.: National Schools Public Relations Association, 1972.

KOZOL, J. "Free Schools: A Time for Candor." *Saturday Review*, March 4, 1972, 51–55.

LEWIS, M. A., KIFER, R. E., GREEN, D. R., ROOSA, J. B., and PHILLIPS, E. L. "The SOCS Model: A Technique for Training *Achievement Place* Students in Complex Communication Skills." Paper presented at American Psychological Association, Montreal, Canada, 1973.

LEWIS, W. W. "Continuity and Intervention in Emotional Disturbance: A Review." *Exceptional Children*, *31*, 9 (1965): 465–476.

MERCER, J. *Labeling the Mentally Retarded*. Los Angeles: University of California Press, 1972.

MINUCHIN, S., CHAMBERLAIN, P., and GRAUBARD, P. "A Project to Teach Learning Skills to Disturbed, Delinquent Children." *American Journal of Orthopsychiatry*, *37* (1967): 558–567.

The New York Times. Education Page, February 20, 1971.

O'LEARY, K. D., and BECKER, W. "The Effects of the Intensity of a Teacher's Reprimands on Children's Behavior." *Journal of School Psychology*, 7 (1969): 8–11.

O'LEARY, K. D., and DRABMAN, R. "Token Reinforcement in the Classroom: A Review." *Psychology Bulletin*, *75*, 6 (1971).

PATTERSON, G. R., COBB, J. A., and RAY, R. S. "A Social Engineering Technique for Retraining the Families of Aggressive Boys." In H. Adams and L. Unikel (eds.), Georgia Symposium in Experimental Clinical Psychology, Vol. II, Springfield, Illinois: Thomas, 1972.

PETERSON, I. "Columbia Dedicates a Building to Help Teach Handicapped." *The New York Times*, November 25, 1973, 66.

POIRIER, G. *Students as Partners and Team Learning*. Berkeley: Center of Team Learning, 1970.

POLSKY, H. W. *Cottage Six*. New York: Russell Sage Foundation, 1962.

PREMACK, D. "Toward Empirical Behavior Laws: I—Positive Reinforcement." *Psychology Review*, 66 (1959): 219–233.

RABKIN, J., and RABKIN, R. "Delinquency and the Lateral Boundary of the Family." In Graubard, P. (ed.), *Children against Schools*. Chicago: Follett, 1969.

RHODES, W. C. "A Community Participation Analysis of Emotional Disturbance." *Exceptional Children, 36* (1970): 309–316.

RHODES, W. C. "The Disturbing Child: A Problem of Ecological Management." *Exceptional Children, 33* (1967): 449–455.

ROSENTHAL, R., and JACOBSON, L. *Pygmalion in the Classroom: Teacher Expectation and Pupil's Intellectual Development.* New York: Holt, 1968.

SALZBERG, C. "Freedom and Responsibility in an Elementary School." In G. Semb (ed.), *Behavior Analysis and Education,* 1972. The University of Kansas Support and Development Center for Follow Through Department of Human Development, 1972, 62–77.

SPENCE, I. "Counting the Teacher Reactions to Pupil Behaviors: A Tool for Teacher Training." Unpublished doctoral dissertation, Yeshiva University, New York, 1972.

THOMAS, D., BECKER, W., and ARMSTRONG, M. "Production and Elimination of Disruptive Classroom Behavior by Systematically Varying Teacher's Behavior." *Journal of Applied Behavior Analysis, 1* (1968): 35–45.

ULLMANN, L., and KRASNER, L. *Case Studies in Behavior Modification.* New York: Holt, 1965.

WHITEHEAD, R. M. "How the Young Are Taught in China." *Saturday Review,* March 4, 1972, 17.

WITHERS, T. "Attitudes of Teachers Towards Psychological Services as Measured by Osgood's Semantic Differential." Unpublished doctoral dissertation, University of Southern California, 1968.

Index